This Book Belongs to

Bob Davidson

20 Churchfield Rd

Ecdeshall

THE STORY OF THE GUN

THE STORY OF THE
GUN

Ian V Hogg

THE HISTORY CHANNEL
WHERE THE PAST COMES ALIVE

BOXTREE

First published in Great Britain in 1996 by Boxtree Limited

Text © Ian Hogg 1996

The right of Ian Hogg to be identified as Author of this Work has been asserted
by him in accordance with the Copyright, Designs and Patents Act 1988.

1 3 5 7 9 10 8 6 4 2

Designed by Robert Updegraff
Colour Origination by Create Publishing Services Ltd
Printed and bound in the UK by Bath Press, Somerset for

Boxtree Limited
Broadwall House
21 Broadwall
London SE1 9PL

A CIP catalogue entry for this book is available from the British Library.

ISBN 0 7522 1087 4

Contents

Introduction

Introduction

H AVE YOU EVER STOPPED to imagine what the world would have been like if gunpowder and the gun had never been invented? It's a sobering thought. All those "endangered species" of today would be standing on each others' shoulders, and *Homo sapiens* would be the endangered ones! A large proportion of all those animals which have been dispatched by gunfire would have survived and prospered. Come to think of it, perhaps the human race wouldn't be outnumbered – think of all those people killed in wars by gunfire who might otherwise have survived and left descendants. The world would be a pretty crowded place.

Let us forget about killing for a moment. Consider the gun as a piece of mechanical engineering. Just think what a machine gun does. You press the trigger, the gun fires, opens the breech, extracts the empty cartridge case and ejects it, withdraws a fresh cartridge from the feed belt, locates the cartridge correctly in the feed system, rams it into the chamber, closes the breech, locks it and fires the next round. If you sat down with a pencil and a piece of paper, do you think you could design a mechanism to do this for one complete cycle? Yet a machine gun not only does it once, it continues to do at speeds up to 100 times a second! And it will continue to do so as long as you keep it fed with ammunition and press the trigger. There are records of machine guns firing over a quarter of a million rounds virtually non-stop without faltering. If you had an automobile as reliable as that you would consider yourself lucky. So the gun is a notable feat of engineering in its own right.

What language do you speak? If the gun had not been invented would you still be speaking that same language? Or would you be speaking the language of some large and aggressive neighboring country? Did you eat meat today? A gun probably put it on your plate – a highly specialized gun, perhaps, but a gun nonetheless.

The machine gun, master of the field in World War I. Sergeant Wilkinson winning the Victoria Cross in 1916 by stopping a German advance with a Maxim gun.

Like it or not, the gun has made the world what it is today. It has determined national boundaries, determined types of government, fed millions of people and protected millions more from predatory animals. True, it has killed tens of millions of people, but it must be remembered that people were killing each other before the gun appeared on the scene, and if every gun vanished from the face of the earth tomorrow, people would still find some other convenient method with which to kill each other.

This book tells the story of the gun from its mysterious and clouded origin to the place it holds in today's world. It is a long and complex story, and in a book of this length, we can only scratch the surface and trace the most important lines of development. And for this reason, much of this volume deals with military weapons, because it is warfare which has provided the incentive for almost every stage of improvement in the history of the gun. The gun's development has been a curious succession of long periods of inactivity, followed by furious spurts as some new innovation is developed, tried and accepted, and there has been more innovation and development since 1850 than there was in the entire 500 years for which the gun had then existed. So far as sporting weapons are concerned, there has been very little advance during this century, as most sporting rifles use a bolt mechanism perfected in 1898, while the familiar lever-action carbine is even older. This is simply because the sporting rifle, or shotgun, reached a peak of mechanical perfection around the turn of the century, and there has been no particular reason to demand new technology since.

On the other hand, warfare is a constant matter of keeping in advance of one's potential enemies, and therefore inventors and designers, are always seeking ways to make military weapons more effective. Soldiers, too, ask designers and inventors to produce weapons to solve some particular tactical problem, or to improve the performance of existing weapons – make them lighter, make them shoot further, make them shoot faster – and for this reason most of the 20th-century innovations in firearms have begun with a military application. Occasionally, this has spilled over into the commercial and sporting field, but broadly speaking, the changes in sporting weapons during this century have principally been concerned with making them cheaper, more reliable and simpler to mass-produce, and almost all the improvements in this area can be traced back to similar demands placed upon military weapons by the economics of war.

The firearm has produced a surprising number of familiar names – names recognized by people who know very little else about weapons. From the USA came John Browning, Samuel Colt, Oliver Winchester, Eli Remington, Horace Smith and Daniel Wesson, laying the foundations of an industry which later produced men of the caliber of John Garand, Bill Ruger and Eugene Stoner. Britain gave us James Lee, Philip Webley, William Metford and Charles Lancaster. Germany produced Georg Luger and Peter Paul Mauser, Austria gave us von Mannlicher, Karl Krnka and George Roth, Italy came up with Pietro Beretta and Luigi Franchi, and Russia with Mosin, Degtyarev, Simonov, Kalashnikov and Makarov. In some parts of Europe any automatic pistol is "a Browning", while almost globally, any automatic rifle with a curved magazine is "a Kalashnikov". Anybody who has watched sufficient TV or movies can instantly identify a Luger pistol, a Winchester carbine, a Colt revolver or Bren machine gun. But ask them who was Luger or Winchester, or when Sam Colt invented his revolver, or why the machine gun is called a Bren, and they will probably not know.

This book will tell you these, and many other, interesting facts as it passes through the years of the gun, showing how a primitive and ineffectual device has gradually improved until it has become not only a weapon, but an indispensable tool. Make no mistake about it. If the gun had not been invented, the world would be a very different place today.

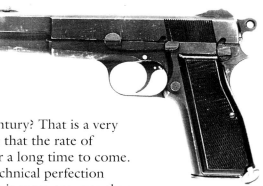

One of the classic designs: the Browning 9 mm High Power of 1935, used by almost every army in the world at some time or other.

And what will happen to the gun in the 21st century? That is a very difficult question to answer, but the indications are that the rate of invention and innovation is going to slow down for a long time to come. Firearms of all kinds have now reached a level of technical perfection which will be difficult to better. Almost any firearm is more accurate than the person firing it, so there is little to be gained by attempting to improve the gun in this respect. Reliability is such that a man can own a weapon for 30 years, use it regularly, and never have it fail him. Synthetic materials and alloys to lighten the weapon have also been applied about as far as is possible, and any further technical advance in firearm design or construction will take a totally innovative breakthrough of a nature we cannot even imagine (if we could, somebody would have done it), and it will take an enormous sum of money to develop and perfect. That being the case, the resulting weapon would be extremely expensive, and the question would then arise "Is the percentage increase in performance worth the percentage increase in price?" And there is a strong probability that the answer would be a resounding "No!" On the whole, therefore, I do not think that there is likely to be any startling innovation in firearms for several years to come.

But you never know – it may just happen that somebody studying this brief history might put his, or her, finger on that innovative breakthrough and confound my prophecy. I wish them the very best of luck, and I wouldn't mind a bit!

CHAPTER ONE

POWDER AND SHOT

A S THE 13TH CENTURY drew to its close, warfare had settled into a routine pattern. The mounted knight provided the mobility and shock elements, while archers and spearmen on foot provided the offensive and defensive striking force. Armies would set forth, pick their battleground and take up their positions facing each other. Archers would then pour in a withering shower of arrows as the knights would charge, relying on their speed, armor and momentum to carry them into, and through, the opposing lines as, with lance or sword, they struck at everything in their way, thus opening a breach in the enemy lines into which the foot soldiers, with pikes, spears and short swords, could follow. While the footmen struggled hand-to-hand, the knights of each side jousted until the victors were able to turn back into the mêlée and aid their footmen to complete the victory.

The legend of Black Berthold, the monk who discovered gunpowder, which is no more than a legend.

If one of the contestants bolted himself inside a castle, then a different set of rules came into play. Engines of war – catapults, mangonels and tre-buchets – hurled rocks against the defenses, and often hurled other things as well, including dead horses, prisoners and balls of blazing fire. A tower on wheels, packed with archers and spearmen, would be pushed towards the wall, a drawbridge dropped, and the attackers swarmed on to the wall and ramparts. Meanwhile, another squad would be assailing the main gate with a ram, so one way or another, the walls would be breached and the castle taken – or not, depending upon the strength and skills of the two contenders. But whichever way you looked at it, warfare was a trial of strength between men, with relatively little intervention by machinery.

All this was simply the perfection of methods of warfare which had been slowly worked out over the previous 5,000 or so years, but the 12th century was to see a revolution which would upset all the perfected systems, change the face of warfare and, in due course, change the face of the world itself. Gunpowder was waiting to make its appearance.

Nobody knows who invented gunpowder – let us be clear about that. Theories abound, but facts are absent. The Chinese, we know, had developed various pyrotechnic compositions, including primitive rockets and simple fireworks, but so far as we can ascertain, they never applied any of these compositions to the propelling of something out of a tube. There are grounds for believing that some of this knowledge moved westwards in the hands of traders and became known to the Arabs, and from there spread into Europe where, in the hands of the medieval alchemists, it was experimented with and improved into what we now call gunpowder. The first positive statement relating to gunpowder appears in a document written in 1242 by Roger Bacon entitled *On the Miraculous Power of Art and Nature*. Bacon (circa 1214–1294) was a Franciscan friar, scientist and philosopher and, like many another, seems to have had the intention of writing down a compendium of the world's knowledge. Among this knowledge, Bacon knew about black powder and, not surprisingly, wanted to include it in his treatise. But as a Franciscan, Bacon knew very well that in 1139 the Second Council of the Lateran had issued a decree laying under anathema (a sentence of excommunication) any person making, or professing knowledge of, fiery compositions for military purposes. If he came out with what he knew in a plain statement, he was liable to put his life at risk. His outspokenness had already caused him to be viewed with suspicion as a probable practitioner of the "Black Arts", so he concealed his secret in an anagram which was to remain unsolved for over 600 years.

Even so, he fell foul of the Franciscan Order, and in 1257 Bonaventura, General of the Order, stopped Bacon's series of lectures at Oxford and ordered him into confinement in Paris, where he remained incommunicado for the next eight years. In 1266 the newly-appointed Pope Clement IV asked Bacon for a number of treatises on the current state of scientific knowledge. One of these was the *Opus Tertus* – an encyclopedia of sorts – and having sent this off to Rome, Bacon was allowed to return to his teaching at Oxford.

And that was that, and remained so until the 1880s when British army officer Lt Col H. W. L. Hime, Royal Artillery, began studying the history of gunpowder, and in particular the *Marvellous Power of Art and Nature*. He was struck by the meaningless jumble of words which appeared in the text just as Bacon seemed to be warming towards the subject of fiery compositions, and after much examination and thought, Hime realized that the words were an anagram. After redistributing the letters and adding punctuation, Bacon's secret of 1242 stood revealed – "But of saltpetre take 7 parts, 5 of young hazel twig and 5 of sulphur and so thou wilt call up thunder and destruction if thou know the art".

Hime's publication of his researches led to more students delving into old records, and in 1909 Professor Pierre Duhem of Bordeaux University came across a document in the *Bibliotheque Nationale* in Paris which proved to be a missing part of the *Opus Tertum* of 1266. It contained the following:

> From the flaming and flashing of certain igneous mixtures, and the terror inspired by their noise, wonderful consequences ensue which no-one can guard against or endure. As a simple example may be mentioned the noise and flame generated by the powder, known in divers places, composed of saltpetre, sulphur and charcoal. When a quantity of this powder, no larger than a man's finger, be wrapped in a piece of parchment and ignited, it explodes with a blinding flash and a stunning noise. . .

Notice that Bacon makes no claim to having discovered or invented this powder, but simply points out that it was "known in divers places", implying that such a thing was now common knowledge and he was merely reporting what many people already knew. And note also that all he reports upon is the ability to make an explosion – there is no mention of putting that explosion to work in any way.

The next positive reference comes in a manuscript written in 1325 by English scholar Walter de Millemete. Like Bacon's work, this appears to have been a review of current knowledge, entitled *On the Duties of Kings*, and was prepared for the young King Edward III. There is no mention of guns or powder in the text, but there is the first illustration of a cannon. Shaped rather like a vase laid on its side, it has a belled mouth and a thickening over the chamber end, showing that even at that stage of development, there was an appreciation of the need to put the most metal over the part which contained the explosion. The projectile is an arrow, and the gun is being fired by a man holding a red-hot iron. In the following year the records of Florence, in Italy, record the manufacture of brass cannon and iron balls "for the defense of the commune, camps and territory of Florence", and in 1338 there is record of a contract between John Starlyng, Clerk of the King's Ships, and Helmyng Leget, Keeper of the King's Ships, in which "Ye said John doth deliver to ye said Helmyng ij canons de ferr, un canon de ferr ove II chambers, un autre de bras ove un chamber" (two cannons of iron, one cannon of iron of two chambers, one other of brass of one chamber). From that time onwards, references come, if not thick and fast, at least with sufficient regularity, to suggest that the cannon could not have been known much before about 1320. But we are no nearer to finding who invented it.

The coloring of the cannon shown in the Millemete manuscript suggests that it was of bronze, and the rounded shape suggests that it was cast. This is a reasonable assumption, since bell-casting was a normal practice by that time, and the same skill could be used to cast a cannon. But it

13

A contemporary drawing, showing how the first cannons were used, mounted on blocks and trestles of wood. Notice, too, the short range and the archers protecting the gunners as they touch off the cannons with hot irons.

was an expensive and slow process, demanding skilled artisans and scarce metal, and before the century was out, simpler and cheaper methods of making cannon were being used. The similarity between a hollow cylindrical cannon and a hollow cylindrical barrel obviously suggested the technique of coopering, building a gun up from strips of metal assembled around a former, heated and hammered to weld them together, and then bound into place and reinforced by iron hoops. This also gave rise to calling the basic working component of the cannon the "barrel".

Once this technique had been mastered, the cannon was no longer restricted in size by the imperfect casting techniques of the day, or the expensive castable metal – it could be put together by any competent smith from common iron, and the size of cannon soon began to grow. At the Siege of Odruik by the Duke of Burgundy in 1377, cannon throwing stone balls of 200 lbs weight are recorded, and shortly afterwards the same Duke had a cannon made to fire a 450-lb (204-kg) ball, which roughly equals a caliber of 22 inches. And you begin to wonder why, if 22-inch (55-cm) cannon were available, sieges – and there were plenty of those at that time – still took so long to accomplish. You would think that a few shots from a 22-inch gun would soon make short work of any contemporary castle.

The answer to this lies in the gunpowder, as it was, by present standards, weak. The formula given by Bacon was for 41 percent saltpeter, 29.5 percent sulphur and 29.5 percent charcoal. Modern gunpowder is in the proportion 75:10:15. The materials provided in Bacon's day would have been to no great degree of purity, whereas modern saltpeter and sulphur have been refined to a very high degree of purity, while modern charcoal is carefully made from selected wood, rather than being the roughly-produced end product of roasted wood burned inside a pile of turf in the forest.

Having got his impure ingredients, the 14th-century gunner would grind them individually into fine powder, then mix them in the chosen proportion by hand. This was then shovelled into the gun chamber, where it settled into a dense mass, which would prove difficult to ignite because the ignition flame could not burn into the pile very quickly. So, the explosion was slow and uncertain, and there was a danger that some of the powder might not ignite before the shot had left the muzzle, which would see some of the charge ejected unburned, and result in the shot not reaching as far as the gunner had intended. And powder was not cheap – it was 12 times more expensive than lead, which was twice as expensive as iron.

In fact, the weakness of the gunpowder was probably the salvation of the gun, as the weapon itself was not particularly strong at this point in its history, and a more efficient powder would probably have blown every gun to pieces, thus putting a complete end to experimentation. This was the reason for the use of stone balls, as large-diameter iron shot would have been so heavy that the explosion would have built up into fatally high pressures inside the gun before the shot began to move up the barrel. Doubtless all these things did happen, and wise men restricted their armory to stone balls and weak powder, in deference to the other drawbacks.

But having, as it were, reached the extremes of large calibers, the gunners of the day looked at the result and began to move back towards small calibers. Warfare had seen very little change as a result of the introduction of artillery. There was still the confrontation, the cavalry charge and the surge of foot soldiers. The difference was that now the confrontation was accompanied by a brief salute of cannon being fired. And before these ponderous weapons could be cleaned, re-loaded, prepared, aimed and fired once more, the knights had charged and the foot soldiers were swarming past, so that the gunners never had a chance to fire a second shot. Their only hope for playing a more significant and destructive part in the battle was to make smaller guns which could be served more rapidly – and make more of them. It would also help if they could be made more mobile, as this might give the gunners on the losing side a chance to get their weapons away before the enemy charge over-ran them. For the gun of the day was not mounted upon wheels – that refinement was yet to appear. The gun was simply laid on the ground on a bed of wood, strapped to it by ropes, and wedged up to give some degree of elevation so as to allow the ball to fly a reasonable distance.

Among the first moves towards small calibers and mobility was the Ribaudequin, noted in 1382 as being used by the burghers of Ghent, in Belgium. This was a simple two-wheeled cart with a number of small-caliber gun barrels fixed firmly to it, the latter being splayed out so as to deliver a spread of shot. It delivered a useful sweep of fire, but it was restricted to firing in a given arc, and there was no scope for dealing with the sudden appearance of an enemy outside the chosen field of fire. The logical answer, it seemed, was to take the gun barrels off the cart, fit each one into a wooden holder, and then give them to individual soldiers with instructions to fire them in whatever direction they perceived the greatest threat. And in this way the cannon eventually reduced itself to become the hand-gonne.

The hand-gonne appeared some time towards the end of the 14th century. There is no doubt about this, since the oldest existing specimen was excavated from a well in Tannenberg Castle (not the well-known Tannenberg in East Prussia, but a smaller castle in Hesse, Germany), and it is a matter of record that this castle was overthrown in 1399. Even earlier is a record in the English Privy Wardrobe accounts for 1388 which records "III cannons parvos vocatus handgunnes". Another specimen was found at Vedelspang Castle in Schleswig, Germany, which records show was destroyed in 1426.

The hand-gonne was simply a miniature cannon barrel, cast in one piece from bronze or iron, and attached to a wooden stave by iron bands. The soldier loaded the gun with powder and ball, tucked the end of the stave under his arm, sprinkled some powder into the vent-hole at the rear end of the gun,

Hand Gonnes, depicted in a manuscript of 1475 from Lubeck, Germany.

and then applied a burning brand, or red-hot iron, to this "priming" to fire the powder and discharge the ball. The gun found at Vedelspang has a hook beneath the muzzle, which was intended to be affixed to a wall, or tree-trunk or any other convenient solid rest, so that the gunner had better control of his weapon. He could take a rough aim across the barrel, and by using the wooden stave, move the gun to point in the required direction while applying the fire to the vent. This was easier and more accurate than attempting to support the weapon, give fire and point it correctly all in one movement.

It must have been at about this time that the "slow match" appeared as an improved method of igniting the powder in the gun vent. Slow match was simply a piece of rough cord which was soaked in saltpeter and then allowed to dry. When ignited it burned very slowly, smouldering away, but could be fanned into a bright and hot condition by a few vigorous swings and then applied to the gun. The gunner carried a length of this, coiled on a special holder called a linstock, and thus always had the means of ignition ready to use, and contemporary instructions to the gunner included the rule that "Hee must not, for any account nor prayer, give up a piece of his match to another, that hee may not be found short in tyme of need".

The hand-gonne gradually reduced its caliber and lengthened its barrel until it became the arquebus. The wooden stake gradually took on a more recognizable shape, and was formed so as to carry the barrel securely at one end, and fit the shoulder of the firer at the other. And instead of carrying a linstock, the arquebusier had the smouldering slow match carried in a curved arm on the side of the weapon stock, so that by pulling on one end of the arm, the top end swung down and pressed the burning match against the "touch-hole" of the arquebus and fired it. The weapon, though, was no lightweight, and the arquebusier also carried a forked support which he placed in the ground and then rested the barrel of the arquebus within it while he duly took aim and fired.

With the weapon at his shoulder, the soldier could now take a more accurate aim, and as early as 1450 there are examples of guns with a blade on the muzzle and a block with a central notch at the breech end, across which a quite precise aim could be taken. Not that it did much good, as the guns of the period were still roughly made and the ball was liable to go virtually anywhere in front of the muzzle and not, necessarily, where the gun was pointed, but this was accepted as a matter of chance – hence the saying, "The first shot is for the Devil, the second is for God, and the third for the King". Gradual improvements in manufacturing – especially in the boring out of the interior of the barrel to achieve a straighter and more smooth finish – did eventually lead to guns which shot where they were aimed, and by the middle of the 16th century, competitive shooting had become a relatively common pastime in Europe. Competitions between firearms were arranged and, surprisingly, competitions between firearms and crossbows, in which the firearms were not always victorious.

Loading an arquebus with powder, from the drill book of Jacob de Gheyne published in 1607.

CHAPTER TWO

FROM SMOOTHBORE TO RIFLE

WITHIN ITS LIMITATIONS, the matchlock was a workable weapon, but these limitations were severe. Firstly, it was quite impractical to carry it ready for action for any length of time, as having loaded the powder and ball, you then carried the weapon in one hand while you carried a length of burning string in the other, bringing the two together when the time came to fire. Then you had, somehow, to put your length of string in a safe and dry place while you re-charged the gun with powder and ball, pick up your string, and carry on. And when the string burned down you had to get out a fresh piece and light it, and so on and so forth. On the other hand, if you didn't want to carry the burning string around, then when the need to fire the weapon arose, you had to sit down with flint and tinder and light the string before you could do anything else. It could hardly be called a "quick response" weapon.

For military purposes it was adequate, as you could always light the string when battle loomed ahead. But for sporting purposes – the shooting of game – something better was needed, and some time in the late 15th century the wheel lock appeared. Its precise date and place of origin is not known, though evidence suggests that it came from Hungary, or possibly northern Italy. The earliest identifiable wheel lock weapon, housed in a collection in Munich, carries a coat of arms which existed only between 1521 and 1526, and this is a fairly advanced model. Leonardo da Vinci produced two drawings of wheel locks dated 1508, while a number of primitive specimens exist from the early 16th century which cannot be accurately dated.

ABOVE **A German soldier of the early 17th century armed with a matchlock musket.**

OPPOSITE **16th-century French cavalry with wheel lock pistol and carbine, a sketch depicting the time of Henry IV, about 1595.**

The principle of the wheel lock is still with us in the everyday cigarette lighter – a roughened wheel is spun in contact with iron pyrites to throw off sparks and ignite the lighter fuel to produce a flame. The wheel lock used a roughened wheel propelled by a spring which was wound up by a "spanner" or wrench. A hammer-like arm carried the piece of pyrites, and both were linked to the trigger so that when the trigger was pulled it released the hammer, which fell forward to bring the pyrites into contact with the wheel, also releasing the latter so that it spun under the power of the spring. The sparks were thrown forward into a pan filled with fine gunpowder and connected to the breech of the weapon by a channel. The sparks ignited the powder in the pan, this flashed through the channel into the chamber of the gun and fired the main charge to propel the bullet. To reload, the gunner rammed down fresh powder and a ball, then cocked the hammer, wound up the wheel, sprinkled powder into the pan and closed the cover, and he was ready to fire again.

The wheel lock brought a number of advantages. Firstly, it made it possible to use a weapon with one hand – it needed two to load it, but once loaded and cocked, only one hand was needed to fire it, and so hand-guns could now be made small enough to deserve the name. It could also be carried, cocked, under the clothing and concealed, and this led to regulations against wheel locks being passed in several European states in an effort to keep them out of the hands of the criminal classes. They need not have worried overmuch, as the wheel lock was a precision device, made by expensive mechanics in small numbers, and it was not the sort of weapon that anyone, apart from the rich, could afford to purchase. For this reason they never became standard military weapons and they never replaced the matchlock in the hands of the common soldiers.

The simplicity of the matchlock led to its being copied wherever it appeared, and in many of the more isolated parts of the world it lingered for centuries. A notable case was that of Japan. The early Portuguese traders took matchlocks to that country, and shortly afterwards the Japanese decided that they had seen enough of the rest of the world and preferred to remain independent. They sealed their borders, refused to permit any traders to do more than step ashore, and as a consequence the development of the wheel lock and flintlock passed them by. When Cdr William Perry opened the country up in the 1850s, he found that their only firearm was the matchlock.

The wheel lock, on the other hand, was rarely made outside southern central Europe, which even by the 14th century had acquired a reputation for fine mechanical workmanship, and many of the better examples are attributable to clockmakers. And since they were expensive – and since people who buy expensive things like to show them off to their friends – the mechanisms were often decorated with engraving, inlaid with precious metals, gold-plated, polished and altogether treated as works of art.

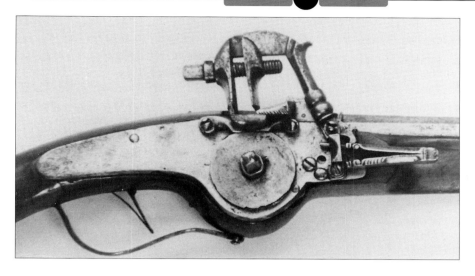

A wheel lock action; the jaws of the 'cock' are open, ready to have a piece of pyrites inserted, and the roughened wheel is below it.

At much the same time as the wheel lock was being perfected, so was gunpowder. We have already met one of the defects of early gunpowder – that it tended to pack tightly in the gun and ignite badly – but there were others. It attracted damp when in store, and it tended to separate into its elements during transport – put a barrel of powder in a cart and move it a few miles and the shaking caused the heavier saltpeter to fall to the bottom of the barrel and the light charcoal to rise to the top, so it all had to be mixed again before it could be used. And when fired, it coated the inside of the gun with a sticky, black and evil-smelling fouling. There wasn't much that could be done about the last problem, but somewhere in France in the middle of the 14th century, an unknown Frenchman hit on the solution of the rest of the problems – he invented "corned powder".

Corned powder, like corned beef, has nothing to do with corn. The word "corned" is now more or less obsolete, but it once meant "in granular form"; i.e. in grains similar to corn, and was probably derived from the German word "kern". Whatever its lineage, corned powder was a major advance, and it was simply made by mixing the usual three ingredients in fine powder form, but with water, so as to make a paste. This was then spread thinly on iron plates to dry, and once this had taken place, it was carefully removed, broken up as small as possible, and passed through a series of sieves of varying mesh so that different sizes of powder could be separated out. But each grain contained the correct proportion of charcoal, saltpeter and sulphur, and no amount of vibration was going to separate them out. Moreover, since the grains were irregular in shape, when they were loaded into the gun there was ample air space between them, even when apparently packed tight, to permit the ignition flame to circulate rapidly and ignite the whole mass instantaneously. And it was later discovered that if you shook the grains in a little graphite or blacklead, then

21

they were given a polished coating which helped to repel moisture – thus, the powder also retained its strength better in a damp atmosphere.

There was, though, one fundamental drawback to the new corned powder – it was too powerful for most of the existing guns. The superior ignition and more even mixture increased the power of gunpowder by a considerable degree, and old guns hammered together from strip iron and bound with cowhide, or cast from inferior metal, disintegrated under the force. So the old "serpentine" powder continued in use for a long time, while the gunmakers set about finding ways of making guns stronger in order to take advantage of the extra power now available to them.

This problem was not one which particularly worried the man with the hand gun, as this weapon was generally made with a very generous safety factor, and by slightly reducing his load of powder, the hand-gunner could get the benefits of corned powder without hazarding the weapon. What did worry him, however, was that no matter how good the corned powder might be, it still filled his barrel with fouling, and after a few shots he had to stop and scour out the weapon, otherwise the fouling became so thick that it was impossible to load the ball, even though the windage – the difference in diameter between the ball and the inside of the barrel – was fairly generous. This windage allowed the ball to be loaded with moderate fouling, but it also allowed a good deal of the propelling gas to escape around the sides of the shot, and since it also meant that the ball was bouncing from side to side as it went up the barrel, instead of being perfectly centred, accuracy and range were badly affected as well.

All this led somebody – and custom generally attributes it to one Gaspard Zollner or Kollner of Vienna – to reason that if he cut a couple of straight grooves on the inside of the barrel, then the fouling would probably tend to gather there, and if he cut down the windage to a minimum then the ball would be better centered, and would also sweep the fouling into the grooves as it went up the bore. Guns incorporating this system were duly made, and soon proved the truth of the argument by shooting further and more accurately – to such an extent that in shooting competitions in Switzerland in the middle of the 16th century, contestants with this type of weapon were forbidden to shoot against plain, smooth-bored, guns and could only compete against similar weapons.

Shortly after that another gunsmith – and legend says that this was August Kutter of Nuremberg – recalled that the best archers would cant the feathers on their arrows so that the arrow took up spin as it flew, claiming that this improved accuracy. So perhaps adding spin to a musket ball might also improve the gun's accuracy. And after thinking about this for a while, he hit on the idea of modifying the straight grooves within the barrel by giving them a twist. He then made the ball a tight fit, so that it "engraved" into the grooves as he rammed it into the barrel, and, since the explosion of the powder working against the relatively soft lead of the ball

A 17th-century arquebusier with his matchlock and firing rest.

tended to expand it slightly, it was engraved even more tightly on the way out. It therefore had to take up the rotation forced upon it by the twist of the grooves, and it emerged spinning. Moreover, because of the sealing effect of the ball being expanded into the grooves, there was practically no escape of gas, and since the ball was effectively supported on the non-rifled parts of the barrel, it was perfectly centred, and thus flew accurately.

As with the wheel lock, rifling began as a refinement for rich sportsmen, but since it was unlikely to break down or go wrong like a wheel lock mechanism, and since it obviously improved the efficiency of the firearm, then there was an obvious incentive for it to be adopted for military use. The principle appears to have been adopted for infantry muskets by the Danes in about 1610, and it soon spread to Germany and France. But for all the obvious advantages, there was one obvious disadvantage – a rifled arm was, in comparison with a smoothbore, expensive and slow to manufacture, which didn't much matter when you were buying one for shooting for the "pot", but mattered a great deal when you had to contemplate buying them by the thousand to outfit an army – so the rifle remained in the minority. Not only were economics against it, but, not for the first time, armies were presented with a solution to a problem which, so far as they could see, didn't exist. Why did you want a rifle anyway? Accuracy? Who needs accuracy? As one English statesman pointed out, "It is not a matter of hitting a particular button on an enemy's coat but of driving home effective musket fire into a packed body of infantry". In other words, at the ranges involved in the warfare of the time, and with tactics that simply consisted of maneuvering two solid masses of soldiers into position opposite each other at about 150 yards apart, and then letting them blast away until one side gave way, there wasn't a great deal of call for the sort of accuracy that rifled weapons could produce.

What was more important to the military was to find some cheap and reliable system of ignition which would replace the matchlock. By the 16th century some progress had been made in the form of a "snapping matchlock". Instead of simply holding a length of burning string and then applying it to the touch-hole on the firearm, an S-shaped piece of steel was pivoted on the side of the stock, connected to a spring and held by a trigger. It also held a length of burning match. On the side of the gun barrel was a dished "pan" connected to the gun chamber by a vent passage. This was filled with powder when the weapon was loaded, and when the trigger was pulled, so the burning match was "snapped" down into the pan to fire. It wasn't instantaneous, but it was quite rapid, and it now became possible to take some pains over the aiming of the weapon, so that rudimentary sights began to appear on the military arquebus – not much more than a notch filed in the top of the breech so that a sight could be taken "across the metal", but considering the inherent inaccuracy of the arquebus, good enough to get the shot in the right parish. But the snapping matchlock still meant marching about with a smoldering match, and also meant that warfare in the wet was almost impossible. Which was why archers, pikemen and swordsmen still formed a sizeable part of any army. Firearms were a "fair-weather weapon".

Flint and steel had been used as a means of striking fire for hundreds of years, and so it is hardly surprising than some enterprising gunmaker – what little evidence there is suggests that he might have been German – found a way of applying the idea to the firing of a gun. In the latter part of the 16th century the snaphance lock appeared. The term snaphance is believed to be derived from the Dutch "snap Haens", meaning "hen thief", although there is also a school of thought that claims it came from the German "Schnapphahn" for "snapping hammer". Whatever the origin of the name, the snaphance soon spread through Europe from Scandinavia to Spain, and beyond.

The snaphance consisted of a hammer, or "cock", with screw jaws, into which a piece of shaped flint was locked. This hammer was driven by a spring and controlled by a trigger. Ahead of the hammer, in a carefully calculated place, was the pan and the vent running to the barrel chamber. The pan was provided with a hinged or sliding cover so that it could be loaded and then covered, stopping the powder from either falling out or being ruined by rain. Ahead of the pan was another hinged arm, the end of which was turned up at a suitable angle. This arm – the frizzen – could be swung forward out of the way, whereupon the gun could not be fired. When ready to fire the frizzen was swung back to lie in front of the hammer, and the pan cover was opened. The firer took aim and pressed the trigger, the hammer flew forward and the piece of flint struck the face of the upturned end of the frizzen, striking sparks which flew into the pan and fired the powder. The firer now swung the frizzen forward again and reloaded the weapon and re-primed the pan, before closing the pan cover. With the frizzen forward, even if he accidentally pulled the trigger there was no danger, since the hammer would fall without striking fire.

As the snaphance spread, so it took on slightly different forms in various places. In Scandinavia, for example, the hammer took on a curved, swan-neck form quite unlike the sharper curve seen in German locks. The Spaniards developed a "half cock" position for the mechanism, which meant that as the hammer was drawn back, a spring-loaded bolt slid across beneath it so that if the firer accidentally let slip the hammer, it would not descend far enough to strike the frizzen, and he could take another grip and do the job properly. As the hammer reached the full cock position, so another bolt slid in place to hold it there, and when the trigger was pressed, both bolts were withdrawn to allow a free fall. This gave the weapon a very desirable safety device. Previously, once the gun was loaded, the pan could not be charged and closed unless the hammer was drawn back, and once the pan was charged the hammer could not be fully lowered. So putting a half-cock position on the hammer allowed the hammer to be drawn back sufficiently to load and charge, and then allowed the frizzen to be folded back and the weapon carried in perfect safety, since trigger pressure could not release the half-cock bolt until the hammer was fully cocked.

Another idea which came from Spain was to form the frizzen as the pan cover, or, if you prefer, make the pan cover into the frizzen by turning up the rear edge to intercept the falling hammer. When the flint struck the frizzen, the shape of the upturned end caused sparks to strike and also caused the cover to be knocked open so that the sparks went into the pan. This was convenient in that the firer no longer had to remember to swing the frizzen back before he pressed the trigger, and it also explains why the Spaniards went to the trouble of devising the half-cock safety device.

After some 50 years or so of gradually accumulated experience with the snaphance lock, it was the French who prompted the next advance in gun technology by gathering together all the good ideas and throwing out the bad ones, and in about 1620 produced the French lock, which was there-after always known simply as the flintlock. The basic features which distin-guish a flintlock from its snaphance predecessor are firstly that the frizzen and pan cover are in one piece, retained in position by a strong spring, and second, that the "sear", or releasing catch controlled by the trigger, moves vertically and engages in a disc or cam called the "tumbler" attached to the hammer. This tumbler has two notches to give half and full cock positions and the mechanism is entirely concealed inside a lock plate on the side of the gun. The result was that the trigger worked on the

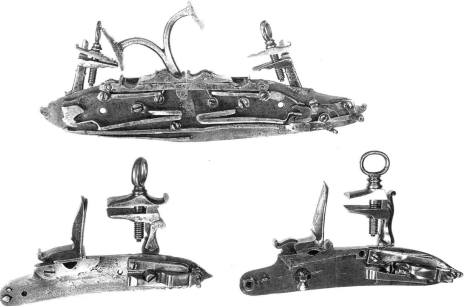

Examples of snaphance locks; the upper is a double lock for a double-barreled shotgun, while the lower pair are Spanish locks.

sear, and the sear worked on the tumbler, rather than the trigger controlling a cross-bolt engaging directly with the hammer.

The flintlock had the virtues of simplicity, reliability and relative cheapness, making it ideal for military service, and by the end of the 17th century it had almost entirely replaced the matchlock, except in some out-of-the-way places. It also brought about a major industry in the production of gun flints – Brandon, in England, Cher in France, the Southern Tyrol and Transylvania were all noted for the quality of their flints, and they were shipped around the world by the barrel-load. A quality flint was generally considered to be good for about 50 shots, after which it was discarded, since attempting to put a new edge on it was a highly skilled business which few, other than the flint miners and "knappers", could perform. Even fitting the flint into the gun was a skilled job, as this extract from the British Army's *Exercises of the Firelock* details:

> In fixing flints, no uniform mode should be attempted; the flat side must be placed upwards or downwards according to the size and shape of the flint and also according to the proportion which the cock bears in height to the frizzen, which varies in different muskets. This is observed by letting the cock gently down and observing where the flint strikes the frizzen, which ought to be at a distance of about one-third from the top. Most diligent observation ought at the same time to be made whether every part of the edge of the flint comes into contact with the frizzen so as to strike out fire from the whole surface. Each particular flint, therefore, requires its own particular mode of fixing so as to accommodate it to the particular proportions and conformations of each lock. Whenever a piece has been fired the first opportunity should be taken to examining whether the flint remains good, and fixed as it ought to be, and no time should be lost in correcting whatever may be found amiss. . .

At the same time as the snaphance was developing into the flintlock, another significant step was being made. From the earliest days of the weapon, the gunner had carried a powder-horn and some bullets – the latter he frequently cast himself, using a simple mould and melting lead over any convenient fire when he had the time to spare. He then whiled away some more spare time by trimming off the "flash" where the mould faces allowed a little seepage of lead, so that he eventually had a fairly smooth, more-or-less round, ball. To load, he sifted a measured quantity of powder into the barrel, followed it up with the ball covered in cloth wad or partly-wrapped in a piece of greased rag. After that he put more powder into the pan, and then with matchlock or flint, fired the weapon.

This was a ponderous business at the best of times, and when the wheel lock came along and allowed a mounted man to carry a primed and

cocked weapon, reloading in the saddle, while trying to control a horse and keep up with the battle became well-nigh impossible. And so sometime around 1560, an unknown genius thought of packing the measured load of powder into a cylinder of paper, so that a number of prepared cartouches could be carried in a pouch, with bullets in another pouch. Loading then became a matter of ripping the end off the cartouches, sprinkling some powder in the pan, tipping the rest down the barrel, crunching up the paper and putting that into the barrel as a wad, before ramming the bullet down on top of the paper.

The next step was to produce a complete cartouche in which the ball was wrapped in the same paper tube, separated from the powder by a thread tied around under the ball. With every soldier carrying his ammunition in the same form, it now became possible to reduce the business of loading to a drill which, with sufficient instruction, even the most stupid recruit could follow:

> Upon the command "Prime and Load", make a quarter turn to the right, at the same time bringing the firelock down to the priming position. . . Open the pan.
> "Upon the command 'Handle Cartridge', first, draw the cartridge from the pouch. Second, bring it to the mouth, holding it between the forefinger the thumb, and bite off the top of the cartridge.
> "Upon the command 'Prime', first, shake out some powder into the pan. and place the last three fingers on the hammer. Second, shut the pan.

A French drawing which purports to show soldiers of the 17th century with their weapons, but such ornately decorated and complex firearms would rarely have been seen in the hands of soldiers.

"Upon the command 'About', turn the piece nimbly round to the loading position. . . Place the butt upon the ground without noise, raise the elbow square with the shoulder and shake the powder into the barrel. . . Place the bullet and paper into the muzzle.

"Upon the command 'Draw Ramrods', first, force the ramrod half out and seize it back-handed exactly in the middle. Second, draw it entirely out, turning it at the same time to the front and place one inch into the barrel.

"Upon the command 'Ram Down the Cartridge', push the bullet well down to the bottom and give it two very quick strokes with the ramrod. . .

Once the recruit had mastered that, he could go on to learn the "Present" and "Fire". Note that there was no command to "take aim" – he merely pointed the thing in the direction of the enemy, looked across the top of the barrel to check that it was roughly lined up and then fired on the word of command. A company of infantry was generally 100-men strong, positioned on the battlefield in two ranks facing the enemy. The front rank knelt and the rear rank stood, firing alternate volleys on command, and driving 50 three-quarter inch balls of lead into the enemy ranks with every volley. And both sides adopted the same formation, so that each was presented with a target approximately 50 yards wide and two high – difficult to miss, even with a smoothbore flintlock musket.

But this degree of precision and disciplined force was not attained overnight. In the first place, although the flintlock had undoubted advantages over the matchlock, it was many years before the latter was completely replaced, and while armies consisted of a mixture of flintlocks, matchlocks and pikemen, concerted action was difficult to achieve. Moreover, there was at first no standard pattern of firearm. Muskets were purchased as and when required from commercial gunmakers, and no two were exactly the same. Not only would there be minor differences between muskets made by the same man, there would be quite considerable differences in muskets made by three or four different sources – so much so that there could, for example, be no common ammunition supply. The soldier had his bullet mould, and made rounds in his spare time, as the chances of borrowing ammunition from his neighbor in battle were few – in the first place the neighbor would be unlikely to have enough to spare, and in the second place it probably wouldn't fit.

All this became apparent as time went by, and as standing armies came into existence in the 17th century, so governments set about standardizing weapons so as to simplify supply. The exact system varied from country to country, but the English system is fairly representative. After deciding that a musket was needed, the War Office would canvass manufacturers with a broad specification covering caliber, weight and length, and then await samples. Of the designs submitted, all would be tested and one would be selected as the future arm. This would then be ceremoniously "sealed" – literally. A linen label with the official name of the weapon would be tied to the sample and the Master-General of the Ordnance's Seal impressed on it in wax. Thereafter, any manufacturer obtaining a contract to make muskets would visit the Pattern Room and inspect the Sealed Pattern, take measurements and make drawings from it, and then go away and make it. He then brought the first one back to be checked against the Sealed Pattern, and once that was done, he was allowed to get on with making the musket. The system has changed during the past century, but the Pattern Room still exists and the old Sealed Patterns are still there, forming the foundation of an unrivalled collection of the world's firearms.

As a result of this system, by the middle 1700s some standardized forms of military musket were in use which were destined to remain in the inventory for over a century. The English Brown Bess is well-known, though the name is loosely applied to any musket made between 1720 and 1840, and actually covers four different models. The Long Land Service Musket was the first, with its 46-inch (1.16-m) barrel and brass fittings, and it was in production from about 1710 to 1725. It was followed by the Short Land Service, with a 42-inch (1.066-m) barrel. The sudden expansion of the army at the start of the Napoleonic Wars set up a demand which could not be met by the manufacturers, and numbers of the East India Company 39-inch barrel musket were bought and adopted as the India Model. Once the initial orders had been met, a new Brown Bess in the form of the New Land Musket appeared in 1802, and saw out the remainder of the flintlock era. All these were of .75-inch (19-mm) caliber, and came with a 17-inch (43-cm) bayonet, so that once the volleys had been fired and the enemy were getting too close to allow time for reloading, the bayonet went onto the muzzle of the rifle and everybody became a pikeman.

Why the name Brown Bess? Why not? The soldier's best friend has always been his personal weapon, and weapons very often get feminine nicknames. "Brown" was probably due to the chemical treatment of the iron barrel as a rust-proofing measure, or perhaps the color of a well-polished walnut stock, while "Bess" was derived from simple alliteration. Good Queen Bess certainly had nothing to do with it!

A similar sequence led to the Charleville Musket – the French equivalent of Brown Bess. Charleville is a French town on the river Meuse, on the Belgian frontier, and was more or less founded by the Duc de Nevers in the early 1600s. His regime there attracted a number of gunsmiths from Liège, and they rapidly acquired a reputation for their excellent workmanship – so much so that in 1667 the French Minister for War ordered that all arms produced there were to be reserved for the King. At the same time a new system of procurement and supply set up a Grand Royal Magazine in Paris to which all commanders had to apply to secure

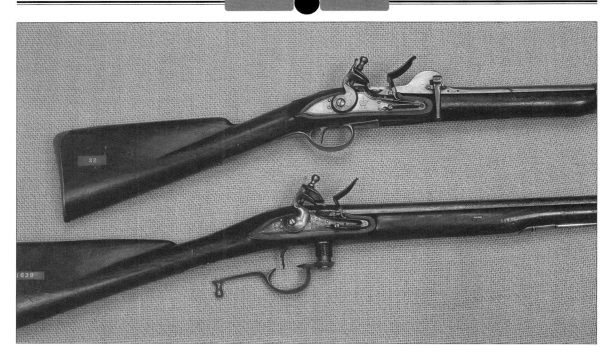

A muzzle-loading flintlock (top) compared to the breechloading Ferguson rifle (below). The breech of the Ferguson is open, the handle beneath the trigger being revolved to unscrew the breech block downwards.

weapons to arm their regiments. It seemed pointless to move weapons across France simply to pass them on, and so in the 1680s Charleville became the Royal Manufactory of Arms. However, a standardized infantry musket was not to appear until the official Model of 1763 was adopted throughout the French Army, and this became the Charleville Musket. With a 44-inch barrel and a caliber of about .70 inches, it was similar to Brown Bess, and since large numbers were supplied to the Revolutionaries in America in 1776, it also formed the pattern for the American Springfield Musket of 1795, which was actually known at the time as the Charleville Pattern musket.

Over the centuries since the gun first appeared, a number of books had been written on the subject, although much of their content was concerned more with the mystique and art of gunnery, rather than with practical instruction. As an example, quoted below is an extract from *Properties, Offices and Duties of a Gunner* by Cyprian Lucar, published in 1588:

> . . .every gunner ought to know that as it is a wholesome thing for
> him to drink and eat a little meat before he doth discharge any
> piece of ordnance, because the fume of saltpetre and brimstone will
> otherwise be hurtful to his brains, so it is very unwholesome for
> him to shoot any piece of ordnance while his stomach is full. . .

But in 1742 there appeared *The New Principles of Gunnery* by Benjamin Robins, and with the publication of this book one can reasonably say that guns, and gunnery, left the realms of the black arts and began to become a scientific study. Robins was a brilliant mathematician and an assiduous experimenter. Before his day, any measurement of a gun's performance was entirely empiric – the gun was fired and the ball went so far, while with a different weight of charge it went a different distance. Beyond that nothing could be said. Robins reasoned that if the ball could be made to deliver its energy to something capable of being measured, he would be able to calculate the energy and velocity of the projectile, and thus have a definite measure of the gun's performance. He therefore built a framework from which was suspended a heavy pendulum consisting of an iron rod carrying a large baulk of timber. The gun to be tested was set up in front of this device and fired so that the ball hit the baulk of wood and made the pendulum swing. Attached to the bottom of the pendulum was a measuring tape running past a marker. As the pendulum moved so the tape was pulled, and when it stopped, there was a measure of the movement. This, together with the weight and length of the pendulum, could now be used to calculate the striking energy of the ball. By performing the experiment at different distances Robins was able to calculate the loss of velocity as range increased, and from this he derived a formula for the movement of the projectile which took into account both gravity and air resistance.

Much of his work was concerned with artillery, but he also used muskets and pistols, and derived various mathematical rules which allowed the performance of weapons to be carefully measured and assessed, and facilitated experiments to determine the best type of charge and bullet for any particular weapon. His "ballistic pendulum", and his tables of calculations, remained the only method of measuring ballistic performance for over a century until the invention of electrical systems allowed more precise measurement.

Robins was a man given to thinking ahead, and one of his most famous observations is worth repeating here:

> Whatever state shall thoroughly comprehend the nature and advantages of rifled barrel pieces and, having facilitated and completed their construction, shall introduce into their armies their general use, with a dexterity in the management of them; they will by this means acquire a superiority which will almost equal anything that has been done at any time by the particular excellence of any one kind of arms; and will perhaps fall but little short of the wonderful effects which histories relate to have been formerly produced by the first inventors of firearms.

The publication of Robins' paper led to an increased interest in the advancement of firearms, and particularly to the development of rifled arms, and this was particularly noticeable in America. In the early 18th century a number of German gunmakers emigrated to America and settled in

Pennsylvania where, because of their previous experience and also because of the interest aroused by Robins, they set about making rifles for hunters and for self-defense on the expanding frontier. Gradually their influence spread and rifles began to be made in Ohio, as well as in other original colonies. These weapons played their part in the French and Indian Wars, in the War of Independence and in the War of 1812 – in the latter affair they were particularly prominent in the Battle of New Orleans. A ballad written about this battle refers to these riflemen and suggested that they were all Kentucky men, whereas records show that the riflemen were in fact from Ohio, and that Kentucky was probably chosen because it fitted the rhythm of the poem better. Nevertheless, from that time onward these early muzzle-loading American rifles have inevitably become known as "Kentucky Rifles", and I doubt very much whether anything I, or any other writer, will say is likely to change it.

Experts on the American rifle divide the production into three periods. The first was from about 1720 to about 1780, in which time the German style of rifle was introduced into America, and then gradually modified to suit the local conditions and requirements. The German hunting rifle had an octagonal barrel about 30 to 36 inches in length, rifled, and of a bore between .60 and .75 of an inch (15 to 19mm) – it was, of course, a flintlock. During this first period the barrel became longer – generally about 40 to 45 inches (1,02 to 1.14m), though longer ones are not uncommon – and the caliber settled at about .60 inches. The furniture was made of American local wood, usually maple which polished up well and had a good grain figure, and a brass or iron patch box with hinged cover was let into the wood of the butt-stock. Decoration of these early models was uncommon.

The second period ran from 1780 to about 1810. Here, the mechanical changes were minor, with the barrel perhaps longer on average, and the caliber slightly reduced to about .50 inches (12.7mm), but the weapons were made to a far higher standard and were elegantly formed and decorated. This change was largely due to the cessation of hostilities at the end of the War of Independence and the gradually improving standard of living, leading to an appreciation of the finer quality of workmanship. No longer was the gunsmith producing weapons for the new country to fight for its life – these were sporting and self-defense weapons in which pride of ownership featured more strongly than patriotic acceptance of a plain, but serviceable, weapon.

The third period began with the adoption of percussion ignition in about 1830, and continued until the gradual extinction of the breed through its replacement by breech-loading cartridge weapons in the 1860s. During this period the barrels became shorter and the caliber smaller.

However, it is with the first period that we are concerned, because this was where the first serious, and extended, warlike use of rifles took place. The revolutionary colonists used whatever weapons they could find, and the Pennsylvania/Kentucky/American rifle was one which well suited their style of warfare, enabling them to stand away from the redcoat muskets and shoot accurately at distances which the British troops could not match – not at first, anyway, but this changed in 1777 when the Ferguson rifle made its appearance.

Patrick Ferguson (born in 1744) was a Scot who joined the Royal North British Dragoons at the age of 14 and saw action in Germany and service in the West Indies. He returned to England in 1774 in poor health and began devising a breech-loading rifle. The basic idea had been patented by a Huguenot refugee called Le Chaumette in London in 1721, and principally consisted of a vertical breech-block with a slow-pitch screw-thread on it, behind a rifled barrel. A handle on the breech-block could be swung sideways so that the screw caused the block to drop down, exposing the chamber. A paper-wrapped cartridge was loaded and a reverse turn of the lever closed the block. A pan on the side was primed with powder, and the usual sort of flintlock mechanism fired the gun. Ferguson perfected this idea, and one of his principal features, for which he obtained a patent, was to cut slots in the breech block screw thread so that it was less liable to jam from powder fouling.

Ferguson had some specimens made and demonstrated them in front of the Artillery Commission at Woolwich in 1776. They approved the manufacture of 100 rifles, with bayonets, and Ferguson oversaw their manufacture in Birmingham, then trained a company of soldiers in their use, and finally in 1777 embarked them for America and the war. Here, their principal action was in the Battle of Brandywine fought on 11 September 1777, where they contributed largely to the American defeat, and the subsequent capture of Philadelphia. Unfortunately, however, Ferguson was severely wounded in the arm and, with his absence in hospital, his corps of riflemen was broken up, their rifles withdrawn and replaced by muskets, and they became normal infantry. Ferguson returned to service, though his right arm was useless, and was eventually to be killed leading a battalion of Georgia Militia at the battle of King's Mountain in 1780.

No more was heard of the rifle in military service for some years, until in 1800 Ezekiel Baker, a London gunsmith, produced a rifle which was adopted by the British Army. This generally copied the German hunting rifle pattern and was fully stocked, with a cheek rest on the butt and a patch box let into the butt. A muzzle-loading flintlock, at first it was produced in the standard .75-inch (19mm) musket caliber, but this proved to be too heavy, so a lighter model of .625-inch (15.8mm) caliber was adopted. These became the arm of the rifle regiments of the British army during the Peninsular War against the French, and they soon confirmed Robins' prophecy, since they gave their owners an enormous advantage over the musket-armed French troops. The Baker rifle remained in service until it was superseded by a percussion model – the Brunswick rifle – in 1837.

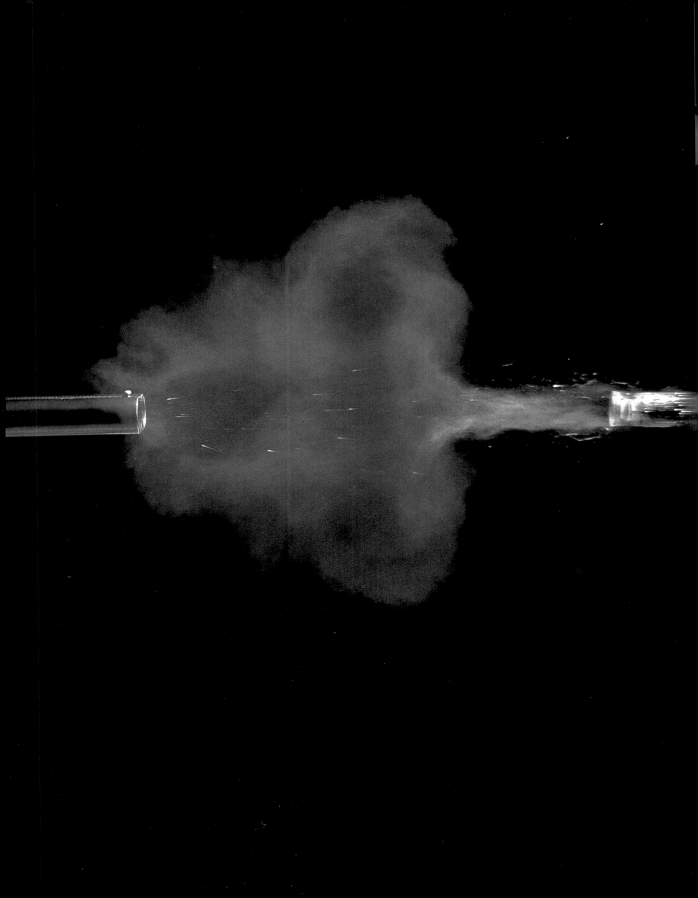

CHAPTER THREE

SOME SIMPLE
BALLISTICS

or

What Happens Inside the Gun, and Why

T HERE ARE A NUMBER of ways to define a gun, but an engineer could define one as an internal combustion engine. When you think it over, it works in just the same way. In an automobile engine there is a cylinder with one end closed, inside which is a loose piston. The space between the piston and the closed end is filled with explosive gas – gasoline vapour and air – and ignited. The burning substance generates more hot gases which drive the piston down the cylinder and, by means of a crank, turns a shaft to drive the wheels.

A gun has a closed-end cylinder and a loose piston, but in this case we call it a bullet. The space between the piston and the end of the tube is filled with a combustible substance – the cartridge – and ignited, and the piston/bullet is driven down the cylinder/barrel. The difference in this case is that the bullet is free to leave the barrel and deliver its energy to the target, rather than remaining captive and delivering it to a shaft.

The energy developed by the automobile engine is generally quoted as being so many horsepower (although these days many manufacturers quote it in kilowatts). It would be possible to quote the power of a gun in similar fashion – the average machine gun, firing for one minute, produces about 200 horsepower – but since we are not applying the extracted energy to drive some machine, this is a pointless calculation. What concerns the gun designer is the amount of energy which the projectile develops, the product of its mass and velocity, and this is generally quoted in either foot-pounds or Joules.

However, just as in the automobile engine, not all the potential energy of the combustible substance actually appears as usable energy at the end of

A high-speed photograph of the shot and wad leaving a 12-gage shotgun.

the operation. As auto-owners know, the horsepower quoted by the enthu-siastic manufacturer is rarely that which appears between the wheels and the road. Most makers take a "naked" engine, put it on a stand, and run it against some load to determine the generated horsepower. But by the time the engine is in the automobile, driving a generator, perhaps a power-steer-ing pump and an air-conditioning compressor, overcoming its own friction and that of the gearbox and differential, a good percentage of the power has been appropriated before it reaches the wheels. Moreover, the explosion of the combustible material generates a great deal of heat, which has to be removed before the engine is damaged. This can be done by forcing air past the cylinder or by surrounding it with water so that the water is heated, cir-culated, cooled and then pumped back to the cylinder, constantly absorbing and taking away the heat. Heat represents energy, and so a proportion of the latent energy is being drained away in this direction too.

Similarly, though with fewer leakage paths, the latent energy of the gun car-tridge propellant is reduced in several ways. Firstly, there is heat – the burning of the charge heats up the gun, reducing the amount of energy left to propel the bullet. There is the friction of the bullet in the barrel to be overcome, there is the friction of various parts of the gun mechanism if their motion is derived from the explosion, there is even the energy wasted in actually accelerating the propellant gas up the barrel, and there is more energy wasted in driving the body of the gun backwards in recoil. In comparison with the internal combus-tion engine's problems, these may seem relatively small losses, but the fact is that the thermal efficiency of a gun – the ratio between the energy theoretically available from the explosion of the cartridge and the energy actually contained in the bullet as it leaves the gun – is in the order of 40 percent. About one-third of this waste is due to heat losses, a small amount to friction and recoil, and the remainder to the potential energy in the expanded gas being wasted as it leaves the muzzle behind the bullet and disperses in blast and flash.

The combustible cartridge in today's gun is rarely gunpowder. As we have already seen, gunpowder has its drawbacks, being susceptible to damp, sensitive to friction and sparks, smoky and depositing a foul mess inside the gun barrel. In the late 1880s smokeless powders began to appear, some more effective than others, and eventually they completely replaced gunpowder as a propellant. In general, they gave the advantages of greater power for a given bulk of powder, less susceptibility to damp, less smoke and less fouling. They have the disadvantages that in some for-mulations, particularly those intended to develop high power, their flame temperature is higher than the melting point of steel, and therefore there is a gradual erosive effect on the gun barrel itself.

The greatest advantage of smokeless powder is that it can be manufac-tured in accurate shapes and sizes which have definite burning characteris-tics applicable to the conditions inside the gun. When the propelling charge is fired the initial burning causes a rise in temperature and pressure within the gun chamber. This causes the rate of burning to increase very rapidly until it reaches the point where it ceases to be considered as simple burning, but becomes an "explosion". By definition, an explosion is combustion in which the speed of burning can be as high as 3,000 metres per second. When the speed of burning greatly exceeds this figure the substance goes into molecular disintegration and we have a "detonation" – as, for example, in the case of dynamite, TNT and similar high explosives.

So the pressure in the gun chamber rises very rapidly after ignition. During this rise the bullet's attachment to the cartridge case is overcome and the gas pressure begins to drive it into the barrel. In the case of a rifled weapon the bullet now has to engrave itself into the rifling, the metal of the bullet deforming and flowing round the contours of the rifling until all the bullet has entered into the rifled portion of the barrel. At the same time, the movement of the bullet has to conform to the curve of the rifling and take up a rotary movement which becomes spin. So there is an axial acceleration of the bullet and also a rotational acceleration, both of which are generating resistance from friction. The pressure behind the bullet continues to rise but, the bullet now begins to accelerate faster and faster, and as it does so it generates space behind itself – in effect enlarging the chamber in which the propellant is burning.

Somewhere in the travel of the bullet up the barrel a point is reached when the space behind the bullet is increasing faster than the evolving gas can fill it, and thereafter the pressure in the chamber and barrel begins to drop, as does the rate of acceleration of the bullet. Some time after this the last of the propellant powder is consumed and no further gas is produced, but the existing gas continues to expand adiabatically until the bullet leaves the muzzle of the gun and the gas can then exhaust itself to the atmosphere. The pressure in the barrel and chamber then drops to normal atmospheric pressure. All this can be drawn as a simple graph known as the "pressure-space curve".

This curve is drawn from the performance we might expect from a simple propellant composed of small solid grains of powder. Smokeless powder has the property of burning at a regular rate on its exposed surface, burning layer by layer until all the grain is consumed. Since the material is impervious, there is no danger (as there was with gunpowder) of the grain suddenly splitting open and revealing additional burning surfaces. This regularity of burning allows the performance of smokeless powder to be predicted with considerable accuracy, and it also allows the designer to change the shape of the grain of powder so as to take advantage of the burning characteristics.

If the "grain" is, say, a flat rectangular flake or a short cylinder, then the burning surface will be large to begin with, and will gradually reduce in area as the powder burns away. Logically, therefore, we can assume that the output of gas will be high to begin with and will gradually reduce in sympathy with the reducing burning area – so there will be a rapid rise in pressure, followed by a gradual drop until the powder is all burned, and this is what we can see in the pressure-space curve marked 1.

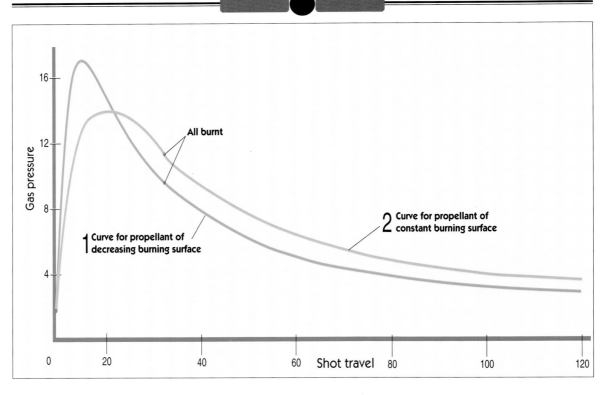

Now suppose we make the grain of powder in the form of a short tube with thick walls. When this is ignited on all surfaces the outer surface will decrease in area as it burns, but the inner surface of the tube will increase in area – one will balance the other, and thus the output of gas will tend to be constant throughout the burning period. This will show as a changed curve in the pressure-space curve No 2. There is, in fact, a slight decrease due to the ends of the tube burning away, but the percentage of this depends upon the length and diameter of the tube, and in the sizes involved in small arms, is not too critical. The length of the tube can be important, since long tubes tend to generate pressure inside faster than it can escape from the ends, and so they split open, giving a sudden increase in burning area and a sudden rise in pressure. To prevent this, long tubes are often split down the side sufficiently enough to relieve pressure, but not making much difference to the general proposition of equal burning areas.

If we take things a stage further, we can produce a grain with a number of holes in it in which the distance between any two holes, and between any hole and the outside of the grain, are the same. When this "multi-tubular" grain is ignited the burning surface will actually increase as it burns, so that the rate of evolution of gas increases. After about 85 percent of the grain has burned away, the "web" between the holes has burned away and the grain then breaks up into thin slivers, each of which now has a decreasing burning surface, but the overall effect is that of a sustained increase. There is no problem from splitting, because multi-tubular grains are always short, their length being about three times their diameter.

You can see, therefore, that by careful selection of the shape and size of the propellant grains, and of the weight of the charge as a whole, the designer can control the burning so that it gives him the pressure characteristic he requires. In a short-barreled pistol, he needs a fast rise and quick burn in order to consume the charge before the bullet reaches the end of the barrel. With a long-barreled rifle, however, it is desirable to generate a slower pressure rise which is sustained for a longer time – a steady push rather than a sudden kick – so that the bullet is accelerated up the barrel and settles down to a steady rate of acceleration and a consistent velocity by the time it reaches the muzzle. Since, as we have already seen, the energy of the gas is wasted once the bullet leaves the muzzle, it is desirable to extract as much benefit from it as possible while the bullet is in the barrel, so it is best to arrange for all the propellant to be entirely consumed – "all-burnt" in the ballistician's language – when the bullet is about two-thirds of its way up the barrel. After all-burnt, the expansion of the gas proceeds at an even rate and the bullet has the remainder of the barrel in which to reach a steady velocity state. In general terms, the lower the pressure at the muzzle, the better the thermal efficiency of the gun.

Considering all these points, it is possible to make some assumptions as to what might happen if some of the conditions are changed. Consider first the effect of reducing the charge weight, while keeping everything else the same. A reduction in the charge will clearly result in a reduction in pressure and velocity, since there will be less energy available. As the pressure will be lower, so will the rate of burning be slower. Thus the effect will be that although the bullet is now moving less rapidly, it will be closer to the muzzle when the charge is all-burnt, and this will lead to inconsistency in velocity, and thus in both the range and accuracy of the weapon.

If we keep the charge weight the same, but decrease the size of the propellant grains, this will increase the total surface area available for burning which is exposed to the evolving gases. Thus gas will be generated faster, and both maximum pressure and muzzle velocity will be increased. The rate of burning will increase due to the higher pressure, and thus the bullet will be further back in the barrel at all-burnt. The limit to decreasing the size of the propellant will be the maximum pressure which the gun will stand before bursting, and it is worth noting that for a reduction in propellant size, the increase in pressure far outweighs the relatively small increase in velocity which results.

Decreasing the bullet weight will give an effect similar to increasing the propellant size. The maximum pressure is lowered because the lighter bullet accelerates more quickly, the all-burnt position therefore moves forward and the muzzle velocity is increased, but the muzzle energy is reduced.

An FBI agent demonstrates the Thompson sub-machine gun. This is the Model of 1928, with muzzle compensator to counteract the muzzle rise when firing automatic, and equipped with the 20-round box magazine instead of the 50-round drum.

The temperature of the charge prior to ignition has effect on both pressure and velocity. A warm charge burns more quickly than a cold one, and the effect is similar to decreasing the propellant size. For this reason, ammunition which is being used for ballistic test purposes is always kept at a controlled temperature, and for the same reason it is never wise to load a cartridge into a hot gun and then leave it to soak up the heat before firing it.

Since the expansion of the propellant gas goes on for some time after all-burnt, the question often arises of what effect the length of barrel has on velocity. If, as we have said, some considerable proportion of the gas energy is wasted at the muzzle, then surely, the argument runs, it would be sensible to extend the barrel and thus put this gas to some useful purpose. The answer to this is simply that there is a length of barrel which is practical for any given type of weapon, and exceeding this in the interest of improving the velocity is a matter of balancing the benefit so gained with the increased length of the weapon, and the probable effect on its practical use. The average rifle barrel is about 500 mm long. Doubling this length would increase the muzzle velocity by only about ten percent, but it would be a most inconvenient weapon for the infantryman to carry in combat. In some cases though, the increase in length can be useful – for example, a pistol with a 100 mm (3.93 inch) barrel performs adequately enough in the combat role envisaged for it. A sub-machine gun firing the same cartridge, but with a barrel twice as long, will produce more velocity and, since the position of all-burnt will be farther back in the barrel, its range, accuracy and consistency will all be improved. Since nobody objects to a sub-machine gun with a 200 mm (7.87 inch) barrel, this is the sort of case where the increase in efficiency is acceptable, but such examples are few.

The efficiency of a weapon can be deduced from the pressure-space curve, since the area beneath the curve represents the energy available at the muzzle, but since such curves are not commonly available, and in any case are useless unless they give precise values of pressure, length and velocity, it is customary to look elsewhere for the information. Thus, the most commonly used measure of efficiency is the muzzle velocity, followed by the muzzle energy.

Muzzle velocity can only be accurately determined by actual measurement, and the usual method is to set up two photo-electric cells some distance from the gun, and a carefully measured distance apart. The bullet is then fired across the top of the cells, and as it cuts out the light in its passage, so the cells produce an electrical impulse which, applied to a timing device, records the time taken for the bullet to pass between the two. This is then applied to the measured distance to produce a velocity, but since the bullet is actually slowing down during its passage due to air resistance and the pull of gravity, the figure so obtained is taken as being the velocity at the mid-point between the two cells, and it is then necessary to apply a correction to arrive at the actual velocity as the bullet left the muzzle. In fact, most ballisticians give a value deduced from the measuring apparatus, stating at what distance the figure applies. The symbol for muzzle velocity is V_0 – i.e. the Velocity at zero distance from the muzzle – but the figure may be quoted as being V_{25}, the velocity at 25 metres from the muzzle. Manufacturers of ammunition know, however, that few people have either the knowledge or the inclination to perform the necessary mathematics, so provide V_0 figures as a matter of course.

Muzzle energy, symbolized as E_0, can be derived from knowledge of the bullet's weight and velocity. The basic formula is $\frac{1}{2} M.V^2$, where M is the mass of the bullet and V the velocity. But mass is not quite the same thing as weight, which is generally all you have to go on, and therefore the simple multiplication of bullet weight by velocity needs to be compensated for the effect of gravity, and since velocity and weight come in different units of measurement, it is also necessary to apply a factor to bring everything into line, and produce a correct answer.

High-speed photograph of an armor-piercing bullet striking an armor plate. On the right, a milli-second before impact and the nose and base drag waves can be seen; in the center, the bullet jacket crumples up while the hard steel core begins to penetrate the armor; on the left, impact.

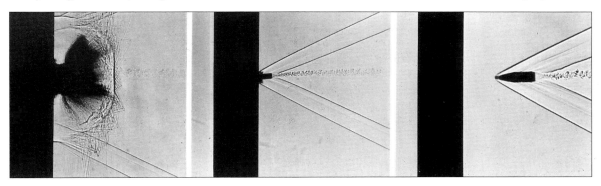

Depending upon the units of measurement, there are two calculations which will give the desired result. For Imperial measurement, with the bullet weight in grains and the velocity in feet per second, multiply the weight by the velocity squared and divide the product by 450,437. The result is in foot-pounds. For metric measurement, with the bullet weight in grammes and the velocity in meters per second, multiply the weight by the velocity squared and divide by 2007 to obtain an answer in Joules. To convert one from the other is simple – Joules x 0.74 = foot-pounds.

As a matter of interest, the highest recorded velocity reached by a conventional weapon is 2,790 metres per second (9,153 feet per second), achieved in 1938 by a German experimenter named Langweiler, firing a specially-made cartridge in a reinforced 8-mm caliber barrel one meter long. The bullet weighed 0.25 gramme and the propelling charge was 11 grammes, the latter having been specially treated to increase the surface burning rate. The maximum pressure in the gun was 176,500 pounds per square inch – as a point of comparison, 40,000 lbs/in^2 is about the average for a modern military rifle.

Having fired the charge and sent the bullet into the barrel, the next thing to be considered is the rifling. The purpose of rifling is to spin the bullet so as to stabilize it and keep it flying nose-first, and the amount of spin required depends on the length of the bullet. If the bullet is too long, no amount of spin will stabilize it, and this limit is in the order of eight or nine times the caliber. This, however, is a purely theoretical consideration, since a conventional bullet of this length would probably be too heavy to reach a worthwhile velocity anyway. But it is worth noting that projectiles longer than this – thin arrow-like flechettes – can be fired from rifles, but need to be given fins to stabilize them.

Determining the angle of twist can be done mathematically, but there are a number of different formulae preferred by different workers. The most simple is of some antiquity, but it produces a workable answer, and is probably used as a guide to empirical experiments. If L is the twist of rifling, then $L = 180 \times d^2 / b$, where d is the diameter of the bullet and b the length of

The contents of a combat shotgun cartridge firing a bundle of flechettes (tiny finned arrows), instead of lead shot. The powder, wads, flechettes, plastic granules (to keep the flechettes aligned while in the cartridge), and closing wad can be seen.

the bullet – the dimensions can be in any unit provided they are all the same. In real life, what happens is usually that the first person to adopt a particular caliber finds out the best twist of rifling by trial and error, after which everybody making a weapon of that caliber simply copies it.

Above all else, of course, the weapon must have the desired effect on the target, and in fact most designers start by considering the target and working their way backwards. It would be an unwise man who carried a .600 Express rifle to shoot rabbits, and an equally unwise one using a .22 rimfire rifle to shoot bear, and it is this difference which has led to something in the order of 400 different sporting cartridges having been developed over the years as different designers have looked at different sorts of game, and developed what they considered to be the most effective means of dealing with them.

The military designer has rather more precise targets in mind, though the matter is a little more involved than might be thought at first. The obvious target is the enemy soldier, but in today's battlefield, he may be wearing body armor, almost certainly a protective helmet (steel or plastic) and riding in some lightly armored vehicle. What is the designer to do?

In fact, the various military authorities have more or less agreed upon certain standards, the most common being to demand the ability of the bullet to pierce a standard steel helmet (the US Army pattern is generally specified) at a specific range. Given this, then the rest of the requirement will probably follow. If the bullet will defeat the helmet at 600 meters, then it will be lethal against unprotected targets at 800 meters, which is as far as is necessary. Gone are the days when misguided theorists demanded lethal effects out to 2,000 meters – soldiers no longer dress in red tunics with brass helmets, nor do they stand in serried ranks. On today's battlefield the enemy is dressed in some camouflage color and hugs the ground, and it is an exceptional soldier who can see a target at 500 meters range, let alone shoot at one.

The energy demanded of the bullet in order to inflict damage against a human target depends, to some degree, upon the shape of the bullet – obviously a slender, pointed bullet will pierce flesh more easily than a thick, blunt-nosed, bullet. But the difference is deceptive, since as long as the bullet has more than 50 foot-pounds of energy it will deliver a blow sufficient to upset the recipient no matter what its shape. Once penetration occurs, then the shape may have some effect upon the severity of the wound inflicted, but even this is not as cut-and-dried as many people imagine, and there are innumerable variables in the science of wound ballistics. Bullet-proof vests can prevent penetration, but the energy delivered by the bullet still has to go somewhere, and the impact can still be extremely painful and even hazardous. And since energy is the product of mass and speed, there is always the seductive argument about reducing the mass and increasing the velocity, so producing the same energy with a lighter weight of ammunition and allowing the soldier to carry more ammunition – or the same amount of ammunition and something else to make up the weight. The proposers of

43

Modern firepower; two British Marine commandos manning a trench during the Falklands war in 1982; on the left, an FN-MAG general-purpose machine gun, on the right the FN-FAL 7.62 mm rifle.

lighter ammunition always promise that it will mean less weight for the soldier, but the soldiers know better than to believe them. It is this line of argument which has gradually reduced the caliber of military rifles from the 0.75 inch (19 mm) of the 18th century musket, to the 8 mm of the late 19th century and the 5.56 mm of today, but now and then voices are raised to point out that although the figures say one thing, real life suggests that as the calibers get smaller the effect on the enemy gets less. This argument will never go away. It must be borne in mind that in military affairs political expediency often carries more weight than ballistic theory.

Once the caliber is determined, the question of accuracy arises. One perhaps assumes that a military rifle will be built to the highest possible degree of accuracy, but this is not so. The military rifle fires military ammunition, and military ammunition is turned out by the million on automatic machines, so that there is bound to be some tolerance in weights and dimensions from round to round, be they ever so small. And unless the ammunition is absolutely to specification, then accuracy must suffer. Moreover, an accurate rifle is one which is carefully assembled by hand from selected components, with minimum tolerances, and which is cosseted and carefully handled – these features will not be found in general-issue military rifles. So the accuracy of a military rifle is something of a compromise between what might be achieved and what must be achieved, and it is generally held to be satisfactory if it shoots to within two minutes of arc. In other words, with the rifle clamped firmly to a bench the bullet must fall within a circle the radius of which is the amount subtended by an angle of two minutes drawn from the muzzle. In practical terms this means that at 200 meters (655 feet), the circle will be about 230 mm (9 inches) across.

A hunting rifle will, of course, do better than this, but even this weapon will be treated with more respect than the average military rifle, and it will probably have been assembled far more carefully, and its ammunition produced to a much tighter specification.

Consistency is perhaps more important than accuracy – to appreciate this point it would be as well to explain just what is meant by accuracy. The accuracy of a weapon is calculated by measuring the distance between a series of shots on a target and determining the exact center (or "mean point of impact") of the group of shots, and then referring this to the spot at which the weapon was actually aimed. If the point of aim and the mean point of impact are in the same place, then the weapon can be said to be accurate, even though none of the shots might have actually struck the point of aim. To take an extreme case, if five shots are fired at a six-foot square target, and one strikes in each corner and one strikes dead center, then that weapon is accurate, since the mean point of impact is in the center of the target, the point at which the firer aimed.

Consistency, on the other hand, means the ability of the weapon to put successive shots in the same place. If we fire our five shots at the six-foot target once more, always, of course, aiming at the center, and all five land inside a three-inch circle up in the top right-hand corner, the weapon may not be accurate, but it is certainly consistent. And turning a consistent rifle into an accurate one is simply a matter of adjusting the sights until the mean point of impact of your five shots agrees with your point of aim. One can always turn a consistent weapon into an accurate one, but an inconsistent weapon, which can be accurate today and wildly off the target tomorrow, is incurable.

The foregoing notes give some idea of the various factors which have to be considered when a gun is designed. There are many others: the best rate of fire for a machine gun; how to keep a machine gun barrel cool; what sort of sights to fit – but the lesson need not be labored. Once the gun has been designed, it will then be carefully made by hand and tested, after which it is generally re-built and modified and re-tested and modified until, after three years or so, a weapon appears which manages to reach the correct balance between all the various factors, and is capable of performing reliably and in accordance with both the visions of the designer, and the wishes of those who intend to use it. At this point it becomes necessary to manufacture it, and this step, from tool-room to mass-production, is fraught with pitfalls. In recent years there has been the case of a military rifle which passed its trials impeccably, but which then exhibited some disquieting defects in service. The trouble was eventually traced to the fact that the designer, in his enthusiasm, had set tolerances and dimensions which the engineering department could not achieve in mass-production. They therefore relaxed some of the tolerances, whereupon the weapon performed erratically. It took a major re-design job to iron out all the wrinkles. And as Josh Billings said, "A reputation once broken may possibly be repaired but the world will always keep their eyes on the spot where the crack was".

45

CHAPTER FOUR

PERCUSSION AND THE BREECH LOADER

THE REVEREND Alexander John Forsyth, MA, LLD (born in 1768), was the son of the minister of the church at Belhelvie in Aberdeenshire, Scotland. He followed his father into the church, and when the latter died in 1791 Alexander assumed the ministry. Belhelvie is not far from the sea, and the Reverend gentleman became a keen fowler, taking his flintlock to the foreshore to provide himself with the occasional bird for his table. Whereupon he discovered, in the most practical way, the principal defect of the flintlock as a sporting weapon.

If you watch carefully, when a flintlock is fired, you can distinguish three separate incidents. Firstly, there is the strike of the flint, followed instantly by the ignition of the powder in the pan, after which there is a short but perceptible pause before the main charge goes off in the chamber and discharges the bullet or shot. And when the Reverend Alexander pulled the trigger on his flintlock, the ignition of the powder in the pan was all that was needed to startle the birds into flight, or movement, and thus evade the shot which followed.

Like many gentlemen of his period, Forsyth studied chemistry and the natural sciences, and in 1799, when Edward Howard discovered fulminate of mercury, he saw that this could be applied to the ignition of a gun. Fulminate of mercury is an extremely sensitive substance which will detonate when struck. Indeed, by itself it is too sensitive and violent to be of very much use, and this stopped a number of experimenters in their tracks, declaring it was too violent to be of any practical value. But Forsyth began experimenting, mixing fulminate with other substances

French colonial troops of the 1890s armed with the Modele 1886 Lebel rifle; a painting by Alfonse Lalauze.

which would moderate its violence, but not detract much from its sensitivity. He tried it as a straight substitute for gunpowder in the pan, but without success, and then set about designing a new form of lock which would confine the fulminate so that its force was directed down the vent and into the gun chamber so as to ignite the gunpowder. Eventually, in 1805, he built a working lock and fitted it to his shotgun. The birds around Belhelvie had a nerve-wracking season.

In the following year Forsyth went to London to offer his invention to the army. The Master-General of the Ordnance was very interested, and gave Forsyth facilities in the Tower of London armories to develop a lock suitable for the service musket, but a change of government brought a new Master-General, who promptly told Forsyth to "be off with all his rubbish". Nevertheless, in 1807 Forsyth obtained a patent for the invention of percussion ignition, and with the assistance of James Purdey – the famous gunsmith – began to produce sporting guns fitted with his percussion lock.

Except for his failure to interest the military, Forsyth's invention was a success. It was widely copied elsewhere, and is without doubt one of the most fundamental principles in the entire development of firearms. Indeed, without his taming of fulminate of mercury, the entire high explosives industry would scarcely have come into existence. He returned to Belhelvie and died there in 1843. Shortly before he passed away, the army finally adopted the percussion system and paid Forsyth £200, followed after his death by a further £1000, between his three surviving relatives – a poor reward, even by the standards of 1843, for such a basic invention.

A wall tablet at the Tower of London commemorating Alexander Forsyth, inventor of the Percussion system.

Forsyth's lock is always called the "scent bottle" lock because of its shape. Instead of a pan, the rear end of the barrel now had a hollow tube off to the right side of the chamber, and revolving around this tube was the "scent bottle", so called because of its elegant, waisted shape. The hollow tube had a hole in the top, and when the "scent bottle" was rotated around the tube a measured portion of priming powder fell into this hole. The bottle was then turned back, and now held a pin above the hole. The hammer, based on that of a flintlock, but without the flint, fell and hit this pin, which then crushed the priming powder in the hole. This flashed down the centre of the tube to the chamber and fired the gunpowder. Periodically, of course, the bottle had to be refilled, but apart from that the system was simple and reliable, though the workmanship of the lock had to be precise, and therefore it was expensive. So before very long, gunsmiths were looking for easier and cheaper methods of applying percussion to the firing of guns.

Perhaps the first alternative was the patch lock. One of the characteristics of fulminate mixtures is that if they are exposed to the air and struck, they simply flash, but if they are confined, even by so much as two pieces of paper, they detonate. And so small "patches" of mixture were stuck between two squares of waterproofed paper – very much like the paper caps which children use on toy guns today. The precision tube of the

Forsyth lock was no longer necessary, a simple drilling into the chamber being topped by a blunt, hollow nipple on which the patch was placed so that the hammer could strike it.

Another popular method was to roll the fulminate mixture into small pellets or pills, using the same technique as employed by an apothecary (pharmacist) to manufacture medical pills, and coated with waterproof varnish. The nipple was enlarged into a cup, into which the pellet was dropped, and the hammer had a small peg on its face which entered the cup to crush the pellet. Pellet locks were soon popular throughout Europe and spread to America, where they were called punch locks.

Manton, the noted English gunmaker, developed a pellet lock, and in 1818 progressed a step further to develop his "tube lock". The priming mixture filled a tiny copper tube, barely an inch long and no thicker than a pencil lead, and the falling hammer crushed the tube to provide the ignition. Some makers laid it into an elongated nipple and crushed it in the centre, while others enlarged the vent and thrust the tube into the nipple so as to strike the exposed end. While theoretically sound, these systems proved fiddly in practice, the tube often blowing to pieces, hazarding the firer, or sticking in the vent and requiring a gunsmith's services to extract it.

The inventor of the eventual solution is widely disputed, but it is probable that, as often happens when the same problem is faced by several equally competent minds, the same solution occurs to several people at more or less the same time. Whether it was Manton in England, Shaw in Philadelphia or Prelat in France, or one of many other claimants, the fact remains that the percussion cap first appeared in the 1820s, and rapidly swept away every other percussion system. The cap can best be likened to a small top hat made of copper. Inside the crown of the hat was a layer of priming mixture, and the dimensions of the cap enabled it to fit tightly around a standardized hollow nipple, screwed into the chamber of the gun. The cap was pushed onto the nipple, and the hammer (with a recessed face which surrounded the cap when it fell so as to prevent fragments being dispersed) fell so as to crush the mixture against the nipple, and thus fire the powder charge in the chamber. Here, at last, was a simple, foolproof and safe system which was inexpensive enough to warrant being adopted by the military, and within the following 20 years, almost every army in the world converted its muzzle-loading flintlocks into percussion guns by simply altering the lock and inserting a nipple into the breech. And except for its use by a few die-hards, the flintlock sporting gun vanished, replaced either by conversions or entirely new percussion weapons.

The general adoption of the percussion cap did not, however, stop a number of inventors trying to improve upon it. They fell into two groups – those who merely wanted to improve the current system, and those who wanted to find something entirely different. The second group were primarily concerned with combining the percussion principle with the other major step – breech-loading. The first group were simply interested in developing an alternative to the cap in the muzzle-loading gun, and as a consequence they were doomed before they began, although some of them managed to promote a workable system before the breech-loaders swept them aside. Perhaps the most effective of this group was the Maynard system.

Edward Maynard was a New York dentist. He had aimed for a military career, but ill-health prevented this, and he instead became a prominent member of his chosen profession. He still was attracted to martial affairs, however, and in 1845 he invented his "tape priming" system in which a long strip of double paper sandwiched pellets of priming composition at fixed intervals. This strip was coiled up and inserted into a recess in the lock of the weapon, and every time the hammer was cocked, a ratchet moved the paper coil and fed a pellet onto the nipple. Down went the hammer, the weapon fired, the shooter reloaded at the muzzle, and when he cocked the hammer, he also primed the weapon. No fiddling around with loose caps or dropping them in the excitement of the chase, or of the battle, as the US Army were so impressed with Maynard's system that they began converting flintlock weapons to the Maynard lock in 1855. As a result, the Maynard saw a good deal of action in the American Civil War. But Maynard was astute enough to realize that breech-loading was bound to come, and he adapted his system accordingly.

The idea of loading a weapon at the breech end was as old as firearms – some of the earliest cannon had the chamber as a separate piece, fitted with a handle so that it could be lifted out from the rest of the gun, loaded, and re-inserted. Given a few spare chambers, it allowed a good rate of fire to be kept up, with one crew loading chambers as fast as they could while another fired the cannon. The problem lay in the joint between the chamber and the rest of the barrel. This had to be gas-tight, so that no propelling power was wasted and so that the gunners were not at risk from flash and smoke. However, a perfect gas-tight fit was impossible to achieve with the crude manufacturing techniques of the 15th and 16th centuries. When translated to a shoulder or hand arm, a tighter fit was possible, but it soon wore away and began to leak – and besides, there was less reason to worry about muzzle loading in a hand arm than in a cannon. Of course, the final problem was linking a flintlock mechanism to a breech-loader, and although it wasn't impossible, it was certainly difficult.

The introduction of the percussion principle suggested that the latter difficulty might now be behind them, and this, together with the gradually improving techniques of engineering and manufacture which the Industrial Revolution had brought about, began to turn minds towards breech-loading small arms.

The birth of the modern breech-loading weapon can be firmly dated – in 1812 a Swiss gunmaker named Johannes Pauly, working in Paris, developed a sporting gun in which the breech was firmly held in the stock and the barrel hinged so that when a catch was pressed the muzzle dropped and the breech end rose in the air, clear of the fixed breech. He then accompanied this with a self-contained cartridge in which powder and ball were held in a paper tube which fitted into a short brass head. This had a hole in the base into which a pellet of priming mixture was placed before loading. Once the cartridge was loaded into the chamber, the barrel was hinged back to the closed position and locked. A firing pin in the fixed breech-piece was struck by the falling hammer and, in turn, struck the priming mixture on the brass cartridge head to fire the charge. The brass head expanded to seal the rear end of the chamber, and Pauly astounded onlookers by firing 22 shots in one minute with his new invention. It was bought by a few sportsmen, and similar guns were made by one or two other gunmakers, but Pauly failed to interest Napoleon in the idea as a military weapon since it was considered too delicate and expensive. He then went to London where, in 1814, he patented an ingenious system for igniting the percussion pellet of his cartridge by using a spring-loaded piston to compress air. This heated the air, and the jet was directed to the priming composition. It never went into production, but the idea was to be revived in the 1950s with some degree of success.

One of the gunmakers who made guns to Pauly's design was a Frenchman named Lefaucheaux. He appears to have been happy with the drop-barrel gun, but less happy with the complicated cartridge and ignition system, and in 1835 he patented his solution, which has generally been accepted as the first really practical breech-loading weapon – the pinfire cartridge and gun. While retaining most of Pauly's gun, Lefaucheaux made an entirely different cartridge in the form of a brass case which carried a percussion cap inside, together with the charge of powder, and with the shot or bullet secured into the case mouth. To provide ignition, a metal pin passed through the side of the case, close to the bottom, and had its point resting on the percussion cap. A slot in the chamber allowed this pin to protrude above the barrel when the gun was closed, the falling hammer then striking the pin, and thus firing the cap. On opening the gun the pin was a convenient way of pulling out the empty cartridge case. Lefaucheaux's gun was instantly successful, and was widely adopted by sportsmen. In 1845 his son Eugene patented a pinfire revolver which was made by several European firms for the remainder of the century. Pinfire bullet cartridges in 5, 7, 9, 12 and 15 mm calibers, and shot cartridges in every bore from 4 to 28, went into production, with some still being in produced until World War II.

The next major advance came from Prussia, where Johann Nikolas von Dreyse and his partner Collenbusch were making muzzle-loading guns and percussion caps. Dreyse had worked under Pauly in Paris in 1809, and in the late 1820s the partners produced a muzzle-loading gun which had a spring-driven firing pin at the breech end, and a bullet with a percussion cap in its base. The powder was loaded in the usual manner, then the bullet, in a cardboard tube so as to keep the base end properly aligned with the firing pin, rammed down on top. When the trigger was pressed a long firing pin, or "needle", went through the powder to strike the cap in the bullet, igniting the charge from the front end. This proved moderately popular with sportsmen, but the military were not impressed, so Dreyse went back to his drawing board and came back in 1845 with the grandfather of all bolt-action rifles, the Dreyse Needle Gun.

The idea seems so logical and obvious today that one can only wonder why nobody thought of the bolt action before von Dreyse, but the action is only part of the problem. The principal hurdle in front of Dreyse was to seal the rear end of the barrel so as to avoid any escape of gas past the bolt, since he was using a cartridge similar to that of his muzzle-loader. It consisted of a conical bullet with a percussion cap in its base, and tied to the end of the bullet was a paper tube of gunpowder. This was inserted into the breech, the bolt was pushed forward and turned down to lock in front of a lug on the frame of the gun, and when the trigger was pressed the long needle-like firing pin pierced the cartridge and struck the cap on the back of the bullet. The necessary gas sealing was done by carefully coning the end of the bolt and counterboring the entrance to the chamber, then grinding the two into a perfect fit. It was a delicate job to get the bolt and chamber joint perfectly gas-tight just as the handle of the bolt turned down in front of its locking lug, but it was done, and the Prussian Army adopted the needle gun in 13.6-mm caliber in 1848. Its adoption was not widely advertized, and very few people realized the significance of the new rifle until the wars of 1864 against Denmark and 1866 against Austria, when the rapid and accurate fire of the Prussian infantry produced victories in startlingly short wars.

Every army in Europe sat up and took notice, realizing that they had to adopt a breech-loading rifle, and quickly. One thing in their favour was that by 1865 there had been some advances since Dreyse had first

The bolt action of the Dreyse "Needle Gun" Model of 1862. The only lock was the bolt handle turned down in front of the lug, as seen here.

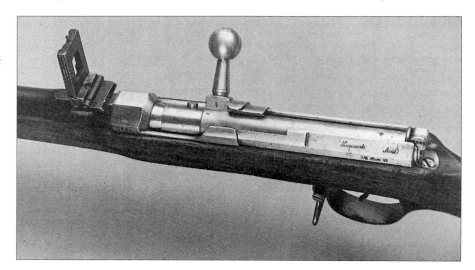

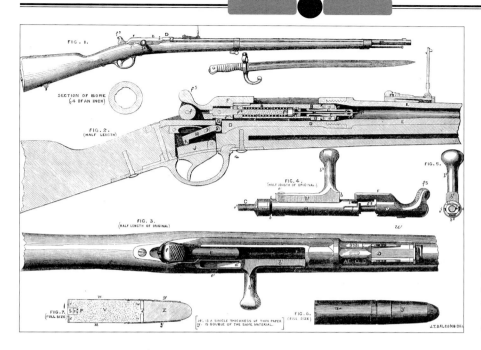

The action of the
Chassepot rifle; an
engraving from the
London Illustrated News
of 1867.

designed the needle gun, and therefore it was probable that whatever they
adopted would be better than what the Prussians had. On the other hand,
it might not! There were a lot of untried ideas floating around the
firearms world, and besides, look at all the muzzle-loading rifles every
army had – replacing all those would cost an absolute fortune.

The one army in Europe which worried most about the Prussians was
that of France, but fortunately a state employee had been both alert
enough to hear about the needle gun, and lucky enough to be in a position to do something about it. Antoine Alphonse Chassepot followed his
father into the gunsmithing trade, and in 1864 was Principal of the government arsenal at Chatellerault. He had already developed a breech-loading rifle, but now, taking the needle gun as his model, he improved certain features and produced a bolt action rifle for the French Army. The
sealing of the bolt was performed by a ring of india-rubber behind the
head of the bolt, and the cartridge was similar to that of the needle gun,
but had the percussion cap at the rear end of the paper cartridge, so that
the firing pin had less travel. The caliber of the Chassepot rifle was 11 mm
– smaller than the Needle Gun – giving it longer range and better accuracy, but the smaller bore fouled more easily. When the Franco-Prussian
war broke out in 1870, pitting the Chassepot against the needle gun,
observers generally agreed that the Chassepot had the edge for range,
Prussian troops frequently coming under fire at distances at which they
could not reply, but since most of the firepower of the Prussian Army
came from their incomparable artillery, it didn't matter very much.

Chassepot meets Needle Gun; French Zouaves and Prussian infantry in a skirmish during the Franco-Prussian War of 1870.

However, by 1870 much had happened in the development of breech-loaders. The American Civil War had begun with muzzle-loading rifles as the standard weapon, but before it was over several breech-loading designs had appeared and had found their place in the battle line. What made this possible was the development of self-contained cartridges.

The pinfire first devised by Lefaucheaux had been improved by Houiller in 1846 through the strengthening of the base and the application of a thick wad inside it to seal the hole through which the pin entered. In 1849 another Frenchman – Flobert – took a percussion cap and placed a small ball on its mouth, developing a small-caliber rifle to fire it. This became popular for indoor target shooting, but was of little practical use for any other purpose. Then in 1854 Englishman Charles Lancaster produced a shotgun using a drawn copper gas-tight case with a percussion cap inside the base. The latter was thin enough to allow the force of the firing pin to impact on a percussion cap inside the base, and thus fire the cartridge, and this can well be considered as the first "center fire" – that is, with the means of ignition central in the base-cartridge.

In 1860 another system was patented in the USA – the rimfire cartridge. This appears to have stemmed from Flobert's "BB Cap" (Bulletted Breech Cap), the common percussion cap provided with a small bullet. These Flobert rifles attained some popularity in the USA, and by making the body of the cap longer and adding some propellant powder. Horace Smith and Daniel Wesson began improving it so that it could be used in their new design of revolver. They then made a fundamental change. Instead of simply allowing the priming mixture to be pasted to the bottom of the case, they formed the case with a rim, so as to locate it properly in the chambers of the revolver and spun the priming mixture into this hollow rim. To fire, all that was needed was a hammer which fell so as to nip the soft rim against the face of the chamber. It didn't matter whereabouts on the rim it fell, as ignition would take place equally well, and the addition of a small quantity of powder gave the .22 Short cartridge a useful improvement in power over the Flobert BB Cap. So by the early 1860s there were three major systems of ignition – pinfire, rimfire and center fire – plus a number of short-lived patent systems, all vying for attention. They were all in their infancy, and the percussion cap was still the predominant system, but the availability of self-contained cartridges, and the constant improvement in design and manufacture, made the development of breech-loading weapons a great deal easier, and led to a rush of designs in the 1860s and 1870s. But now we must go back and see how the development of weapons kept step with the development of ammunition.

One goal of inventors throughout the centuries since firearms had first appeared was the idea of a weapon which could be fired several times in rapid succession, but because the "round" of ammunition consisted of powder, ball and a piece of flint, the problem was practically insoluble. One attempt at a solution was "Puckle's Defence", produced in 1718. This had a barrel mounted on a tripod, behind which was a cylinder containing nine

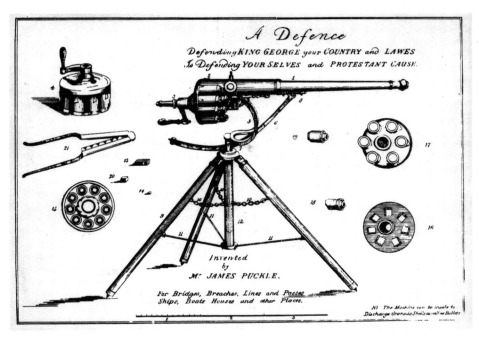

James Puckle's "Defence", a quick-firer from 1718. By revolving the crank at the back, the cylinder could be removed and a fresh, loaded one, inserted. Note that there were cylinders of different capacity, and bullets of different shapes.

55

chambers, each of which had its own pan and frizzen. On top was a hammer and flint. The operator loaded all the chambers with powder and ball, inserted the chamber into the frame and clamped it tightly with one chamber lined up with the barrel. He cocked the hammer and fired, then unclamped the cylinder, turned it to the next chamber, re-cocked, clamped up and fired – and so on. In theory not bad, but Puckle rather undermined confidence in the weapon by announcing that it fired round bullets against Christians and square ones against Turks. In any event, it was never heard of again, and only one specimen exists.

But the percussion cap made everything that little bit easier by doing away with the flint, powder and frizzen. Among the first practical repeating weapons was the "pepperbox"'revolver, which was simply a number of barrels arranged so as to revolve around a central spindle. Each barrel carried a nipple and cap, and the firer had to cock the hammer, turn the "pepperbox" until a barrel was lined up under the hammer, lock everything in place, and fire. Then he had to unlock, cock the hammer, turn to the next barrel, lock up and fire again. And, of course, when he had emptied the weapon he had to set to and load each barrel with powder and ball, and then put a cap on each nipple.

Another idea which appeared in the 1830s was the "turret pistol", best described as a thick disc laid flat behind the barrel and with a number of chambers bored in from the outside. Each chamber had a nipple and was, as usual, loaded with powder and ball. The disc was rotated so that each chamber lined up in turn with the barrel, and when the hammer fell, it fell on the correct cap to fire that chamber. It worked, and reasonably well, but once wear set in there was the constant danger that the flash from the fired chamber might spread and fire one or more of the other chambers. And since, at any time, some of the chambers faced backwards, this could lead to spectacular, if not fatal, results.

These, and similar ideas, had appeared in the flintlock period, but they were more in the nature of technical exercises to prove that the gunmaker was on top of his job and capable of solving difficult problems, rather than being seriously effective weapons. It was the percussion cap that made them possible, and made men think of improving them. One such man was Capt Artemus Wheeler of Concord, Massachusetts, who in 1818 was granted a patent for "a gun to discharge seven or more times". It was a flintlock revolver carbine which Wheeler hoped to sell to the US Navy, but only two specimens have survived, and Wheeler seemed to have made heavy weather of his idea. But he gave a copy of his patent to a man called Elisha Collier, who set forth for England, where upon his arrival he took out a patent in November 1818 for "a firearm combining a single barrel with several chambers to obtain a succession of discharges from one loading". And having obtained his patent, he set about making pistols and rifles to his design, beginning with flintlocks, but very quickly converting to percussion.

The most ingenious feature of Collier's design lay in the operation of the cylinder, which was mechanically rotated and controlled by the operation of the trigger and hammer. Two springs bore on the cylinder, one pushing it forward so that the mouth of the chamber closed tightly over the rear end of the barrel to make a more or less gas-tight joint, and the other was a torsion spring which revolved the cylinder. After loading the chambers and capping them, the cylinder was drawn back, free from the barrel, and then revolved to wind up the torsion spring. Allowing the cylinder to go forward and engage in the barrel locked it ready for firing. Once fired, as the hammer was drawn back to cock for the next shot, a hook linked to it would engage with a lip at the rear of the cylinder, thus pulling the cylinder back and free from the barrel. As soon as it was free the torsion spring drove it round, and as the next chamber came into line with the barrel, so a notch in the lip of the cylinder allowed the hook to come free and the cylinder moved forward and re-engaged with the barrel. As a precaution against the explosion blowing the cylinder away from the barrel, pulling the trigger also moved a wedge behind the cylinder, locking it firmly in place.

The only drawback to this mechanism was that it didn't work very well – sometimes the hook jumped the lip and didn't pull the cylinder clear, sometimes it didn't pass through the lug and the cylinder spun too far. Whatever the reason, by about 1824 Collier had removed the torsion spring and the cylinder had to be pulled back against its spring, turned, and then released by hand for each shot. Collier was not the actual manufacturer – he had the various components made by established gunsmiths in England and ran a small assembly workshop, but in any event the sales of his weapons were not good, and in 1828 he gave up the gun business and went into civil engineering.

But as Collier gave up, another figure was waiting in the wings for his turn, working on his own idea of how a revolver should work. Samuel Colt was born in Hartford, Connecticut, in 1814. By 1830 he was cabin boy on the sailing ship *Corvo* where, according to legend, he passed what spare time he had by whittling a revolver in wood. It's a nice tale, but no more than that, having been invented by the Colt publicity agents in later years. After his discharge from the sea, Samuel joined a traveling show as "Doctor Coult", earning his keep by selling patent medicines and administering laughing gas to incredulous yokels. Although he never had any mechanical training, he nevertheless had an interest in pistols, and with the proceeds of his medicine show, he engaged a mechanic, John Pearson of Baltimore, to build a prototype pistol to Colt's design. Pearson made a number of pistols, each improving on the last, and eventually, when he had a working pistol which he liked, Colt took ship to England to take out English Patent No 6909 of 22 October 1835. He then returned to the USA to take out US Patent 9430X of 25 February 1836. He was just 21 years of age.

Having obtained his patents, he now got financial backing and set up a factory at Paterson, New Jersey, calling his company the Patent Firearms

Manufacturing Co. He was astute enough to hire gunsmith Pliny Lawton to manage the factory while he busied himself where his best talents lay – in organizing, advertising, promotion and sales.

If we examine Colt's design, it can be seen that very little of it was original. For example, the use of a pawl attached to the hammer acting on a ratchet on the rear end of the cylinder had first been used in the 17th century. Colt's principal contribution was to take a number of existing features and bring them together in an harmonious and elegant mechanical whole and, broadly speaking, lay down the shape which the revolver was to take for the future. He was also ingenious in getting patent protection for all these features, something which the original inventors had neglected to do. Since no prior claim existed, Colt was able to obtain a master patent, and having done so took good care to make it stick. Anyone attempting to make a revolver using mechanical devices to revolve the cylinder soon found himself on the receiving end of a writ from Colt's lawyers.

The first Colt revolver (he also made shotguns and rifles, all based on the same repeating principle) went into production late in 1836, and is known variously as the Texan, from its principal destination, or the Paterson from the location of the factory. Of .34-inch (8.6-mm) caliber, it had a 5.5-inch octagonal barrel and a five-shot cylinder. The nipples were recessing into the rear of the cylinder, which was mounted on a central pin attached to the butt frame. The cylinder was slipped into place on this pin and then the barrel – a separate piece – was fitted on to the front end of the butt frame and locked there by a wedge. The hammer was cocked by drawing it back with the thumb, which

Colt's "Third Model Dragoon" revolver in .44 caliber, together with a portrait of Samuel Colt.

also revolved the cylinder and brought a chamber in line with the barrel and a capped nipple in line with the hammer. The trigger was folded up beneath the frame, but the act of cocking caused it to spring out into the firing position – there was no trigger guard. The Paterson was never intended to be a military weapon, but it found favour among the Texas Rangers.

In 1839 Colt improved the design by fitting a hinged ramrod beneath the barrel, allowing the chambers to be loaded without removing the cylinder from the gun, though it was still quicker to carry a pre-loaded cylinder and, having emptied the gun, knock out the wedge, remove the barrel and empty cylinder, slip on the freshly-loaded cylinder and replace the barrel and wedge.

However, the demand for Colt's new revolver was less than he had antici-pated, and when his financial backer went bankrupt, Colt's company was forced into liquidation. He turned to other things, designing an electric tele-graph apparatus and a submarine mine system for the US Army, but the out-break of the Mexican War in 1846 caused a sudden demand for military arms, and Gen Zachary Taylor, who had been impressed with the quality of the Colt revolvers used by several of his officers, sent Capt Sam Walker to see Colt, and arrange for the manufacture of a military revolver. Walker made some suggestions based on his experience with the Paterson pistol, and Colt drew up a design, and in January 1847 he was given an order for 1,000 pistols. With no factory of his own, Colt turned to Eli Whitney, a noted gun-maker and mechanic, and sub-contracted the order to him. Whitney is often called "the father of mass-production", and his grasp of the need for stan-dardization of parts and the concept of using machine tools to ensure inter-changeability of parts, instead of making each weapon as an individually hand-fitted item, did a great deal to speed up manufacture, bring down prices, and organize the firearms industry so that, among other things, it was able to meet the challenge thrown at it 15 years later by the Civil War.

TOP **The Colt "Paterson" or "Texas" revolver of 1842. It used a five-chambered cylinder, and the trigger could be folded away when not required, flicking out into the ready position when the hammer was cocked.**

ABOVE **Samuel Colt's original 1835 drawings for a ten-chambered revolver; he later changed this to six chambers so that a larger caliber could be used.**

59

A Colt "Walker" .44 caliber revolver dated 1847; this is one of the pair numbered 1009 and 1010 which was made specifically for Captain Sam Walker of the Texas Rangers, whose ideas and suggestions were incorporated into the design by Samuel Colt.

The new pistol – officially the Model of 1847, and unofficially the "Whitneyville Walker" model, named after its place of manufacture and the guiding spirit behind it – was one of the biggest handguns of all time. Of .44-inch (11.17 mm) caliber, it was 15.5 inches (394 mm) long with a 9-inch barrel, and weighed just over 4.5 lbs (2.04 kg). Stronger than the Paterson model, it carried the folding ramrod under the barrel, and the non-folding trigger was protected by a brass trigger guard. The mechanism remained the same – thumb-cocked and trigger fired – and the graceful curves of the hammer spur and the butt were to become recognizable Colt features for many years afterwards.

A repeat order for a further 1,000 pistols enabled Colt to set up his own factory in Hartford, Connecticut, in 1848. Here, he put what he had learned from Eli Whitney to good use, installed Elisha Root – a first-class engineer – as factory superintendent, and began manufacturing for the commercial market as well as the military. He made some small improvements to the Walker design, calling it the New Model Army revolver, and then scaled the design down to .31 caliber (7.8 mm) and christened it the Baby Dragoon. And, just as production was getting into its stride in 1849, the California gold rush broke, and many of those who headed west decided to take along one of Colt's revolvers as a form of life insurance. This gave a useful boost to sales, and also helped to establish the Colt as the west's premier pistol.

In 1851 came the Colt revolver which is probably the best-known of his percussion pistols, the Old Model Navy in .36 caliber (9.1 mm). It was to the same general design as the earlier models, but more graceful, with a 7.5-inch (190 mm) barrel and a six-shot cylinder – it took its name from an engraving which ran around the circumference of the cylinder, depicting a battle between the Texas and Mexican navies which took place in 1845, rather than from any official naval adoption.

All this time Colt was enjoying the benefit of his master patent, which was to last until 1857, and prevented any worthwhile competition. His English patent, which ran for only 14 years and expired in 1849, was of less value for the simple reason that there was very little demand for pistols in Britain at that time, and it was not until his patent expired that he decided to try and stimulate sales a little by attending the Great Exhibition of 1851 in London, where he displayed a fine selection of his firearms. He also presented specimens to army officers and grandees of various sorts, and generally garnered as much publicity as he could, before finally setting up a London factory in 1853 to make revolvers for sale in Europe. But by that time he had a competitor.

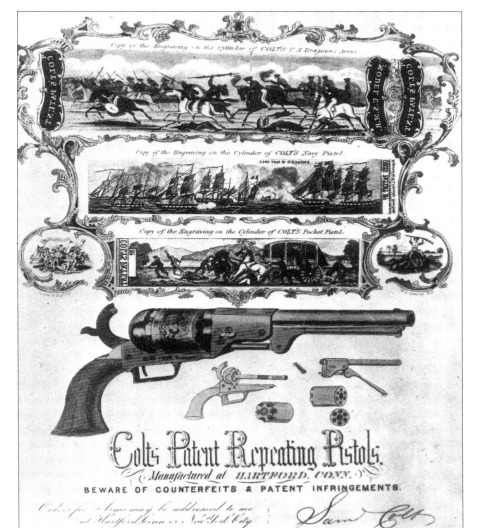

A Colt advertisement circa 1852, showing prints of the scenes engraved on his revolver cylinders; top, the 1847 Walker Colt; middle the Navy model of 1851, and bottom the 1849 Pocket pistol

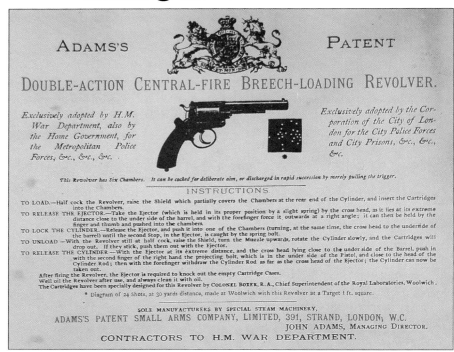

RIGHT **A sales brochure of Robert Adams' double-action revolver; the company title dates it to between 1865 and 1874.**

BELOW **Colt's .36 caliber Navy Model revolver, a highly popular weapon during the Civil War and a design which was widely copied by Confederate imitators.**

In 1851, also in time for the Great Exhibition, Robert Adams, a partner in the gunsmithing firm of Deane, Adams and Deane, designed a revolver which was to become highly competitive with Colt's weapon, and which was, in fact, a much better design. The most important feature of the Adams gun was his innovation of the "solid frame" – the entire weapon (butt, frame and barrel) was forged in one piece, with a square hole into which the cylinder would be fitted, retained by a pin pushed through the front of the frame to lodge in the breech portion. This meant that the barrel was rigidly supported both top and bottom, unlike the "open frame" Colt which was only secured at the bottom. Moreover, the trigger mechanism was entirely different to that of the Colt – the Adams was a "self-cocking" revolver, fired by simply pulling the trigger so that it raised the hammer to the full cock position, moved the cylinder round to the next chamber, locked everything in place and then released the hammer to fire, all in one swift movement. It was this, more than anything else, which caused the Adams pistol to outsell the Colt to military officers.

In those days, officers tended to be in the thick of the fight and they wanted a revolver which was fast in action. They didn't want to cock and then pull the trigger – one sharp pull and everything happened, and that was ideal for a mêlée with rebellious tribesmen. But when it came to formal military acceptance such instinctive reaction came second to formal testing for accuracy, and here the Colt, with the ability to cock the hammer, take careful aim, and then fire with a light touch on the trigger, gave better results than the pull-through of the Adams design, which tended to pull the pistol off the aim. So the initial orders for military revolvers went to Colt, but experience soon showed that the .44 caliber and fast action of the Adams was preferable to the .36 caliber and slower action of the Colt, and after seeing some practical results in the Crimea and India, the British Army changed its mind in 1855 and standardized on the Adams revolver. And in that year Adams altered the mechanism so that it could operate either way – you could cock the hammer with the thumb and fire with the trigger, like the Colt, or you could simply pull the trigger to cock and fire. He had developed the "double action" revolver, although in strict fact he didn't invent the double-action lock, which was the brainchild of a Lt Beaumont of the Royal Engineers, who assigned his patent for the mechanism to Adams, and then went into partnership with him.

When the Colt patent expired in 1857 there was no shortage of people ready to rush into the market with revolvers, but they were forestalled by two astute men named Horace Smith and Daniel Wesson. These two had met in the 1820s and had set up in business making a repeating rifle firing a rather peculiar cartridge which was, more or less, simply a bullet with a hollow base filled with a fulminate mixture. Ignited by a cap, it exploded and blew the bullet out of the barrel, but it was not particularly efficient, sometimes failing to get the bullet all the way to the muzzle, and they were happy to sell this device to a shirtmaker called Oliver Winchester, of whom more later. Smith & Wesson then started looking at ammunition, and eventually designed a .22 rimfire cartridge which, called the .22 Short, is still with us today. They then set about developing a revolver to fire this round, having an eye on the day when the Colt patent would expire. And since they had previously suffered legal problems with Colt, they set about doing a patent search to make sure that they hadn't inadvertently trodden on anybody's toes. During this search they turned up a patent by a man called Rollin White, an ex-employee of Colt's and an indefatigable inventor and patentee. In 1855 he had taken out US Patent 12648 which claimed a number of improbable features, but included among the dross the principle of "extending the chambers through the rear of the cylinder for the purpose of loading them at the breech from behind". White had offered this patent to Colt who turned it down, but Smith & Wesson now realized that if they could license this from White, they would have another master patent which would prevent anyone else from boring cylinders all the way through. So they met White and obtained the patent on advantageous terms – they would pay White a royalty on every revolver made, but they left him the responsibility for pursuing patent infringers through the law courts. As a result of that clause, most of White's profit from the deal vanished into the lawyers' vaults as he fought action after action against would-be copiers of the Smith & Wesson revolver.

As soon as the Colt patent expired, Smith & Wesson were ready with their revolver and their patent, which they enforced rigidly for its full 14 years. No breech-loading revolver was made in the USA between 1857 and 1869 without the payment of a fee to Smith & Wesson. The rimfire cartridge was adopted widely for rifles and single-shot pistols, but if it was a revolver. . .

The Smith & Wesson Number One was a five-shot pocket pistol with an entirely new design – a type now known as a "tip-up" revolver. The top strap, above the cylinder, was attached to the barrel by a hinge pin, and the front end of the frame held a catch which retained the barrel and cylinder unit in its proper place. To load, the catch was released and the barrel "tipped up" to hinge above the cylinder so that the cylinder could be removed for loading. After loading, the barrel was hinged down again until the catch locked, and the pistol was ready. Cocking the hammer caused a "sheath trigger" to pop out from its concealing sheath ready to fire. It was an overnight success, and by 1864 Smith & Wesson were two years behind in meeting orders, and were sub-contracting their designs to other manufacturers to satisfy demand.

The revolver was on its way, and long arms were beginning to follow suit, all, of course, being propelled by first the percussion cap, and then the self-contained cartridge. The Volcanic rifle, briefly mentioned before, was a good example of this. Smith & Wesson had attempted to devise a self-propelled bullet, ignited by a percussion cap, but the propulsive effort generated by a fulminate priming composition was disappointing, so they got rid of the Volcanic to go and do some fundamental research into cartridges. Oliver Winchester, who took over the Volcanic, didn't think much of it either, and he hired a gunsmith named Tyler Henry to overhaul the design and organize production. Henry had done some work on the original Volcanic rifle, but he now gave it a thorough re-design around a new cartridge, the .44 rimfire – he never made any specific claims as to the origin of this cartridge, but since then every Winchester rimfire cartridge has had the letter "H" impressed on its base in his memory. The rifle was a "lever action" pattern – there was a

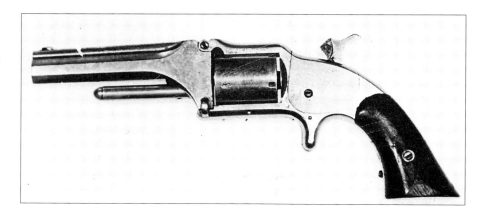

A Smith & Wesson .22 rimfire Model No. 1 Second Issue revolver from about 1860. Some 117,000 were made before production ended in 1868.

tubular magazine underneath the barrel into which cartridges were loaded and in which they were forced backwards by a spring. A lever behind the trigger was pushed down which pulled a toggle arm out of its locked line and drew the breech block backwards, cocking the hammer. Raising the lever lifted a cartridge from the magazine and closed the breech block so that it pushed the cartridge off the lifter and into the chamber. The final movement of the lever forced the toggle back into a straight locking arm, which would resist the breech opening under the pressure of the fired cartridge.

Henry patented this in 1860, and it was made and sold by Oliver Winchester's New Haven Arms Company with considerable success. The only defect was that to load the magazine it was necessary to pull its spring all the way forward and lock it, then disconnect the rear end of the magazine from the frame of the rifle and swing it down so that the cartridges could be pushed into the rear. Then it had to be swung back, re-connected to the frame and then the spring released. In 1866 this difficulty was removed by the King Improvement – a little spring-loaded flap in the right side of the rifle frame. By pushing the nose of the cartridge against this flap it was now possible to load cartridges directly into the magazine from the rear without requiring any disconnection. Later in that year the Henry Rifle with King's Improvement became what it has been ever since – the Winchester rifle. It has gone through many model numbers and has been modified to fire a wide variety of rimfire and central fire cartridges, but the basic design on sale today is still that which Henry and King put together in 1866.

In 1862 the next major breech locking system appeared when Henry Peabody of Boston patented a rifle in which the breech block was hinged at the rear, above the axis of the barrel. Operating an under-lever caused the front end of the block to drop below the chamber to permit loading. This was a powerful action, capable of withstanding heavy loadings, and yet in spite of the American Civil War breaking out, it was scarcely recognized by the US Army and was purchased only by a handful of militia units. Not until after the war was the rifle given military approval, by which time the army had no funds with which to buy new weapons. Indeed, Peabody's mechanism was strangely neglected in the USA, but not so in Europe, where Swiss engineer Frederich von Martini made a few alterations which improved it. First he put in a simple linkage which cocked the hammer as the breech was opened, but then he did away with the external hammer entirely and substituted a spring-loaded firing pin inside the breech block. This was automatically cocked as the breech was opened, and since it had a short movement back and forth, it meant that the "lock time" – the time between the trigger being pressed and the cartridge exploding – was very short: shorter than the time it took for a heavy hammer to fall and drive in a firing pin. This meant there was less chance of the rifle wandering off its aim, and the accuracy therefore improved. The rifle now became the Peabody-Martini, but in the course of time Peabody's name was dropped and forgotten.

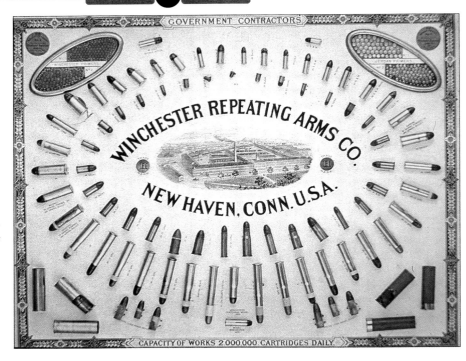

RIGHT **A "Bullet Board" of
the Winchester company,
probably from the 1890s,
advertising the wide
variety of ammunition
then manufactured.**

BELOW **Oliver F.
Winchester (1810-1890)
the founder of the
Winchester Repeating
Arms Company.**

The Winchester and the Peabody-Martini came into military prominence during the Siege of Plevna in the Russo-Turkish War of 1877. Plevna was an insignificant town in Bulgaria, but it was ideally placed to prevent two invading Russian armies from joining up. Osman Pasha, the Turkish commander, occupied the town with 14,000 soldiers, set them to work digging trenches, and with that done issued them each with a Peabody-Martini and 100 rounds for long-range shooting, and a Winchester and 500 rounds for short-range fire. They then awaited the Russians, who duly arrived to be met with a storm of fire which cut down 8,000 troops. The Russians then began a siege, but wearying of this, tried another assault, which cost them a further 18,000 casualties. That stifled their enthusiasm, and they settled down to besiege Osman and his men until starvation drove the Turks out six months later.

The introduction of metallic cartridges had put the armies of the world into an uproar. Obviously, they had to re-equip their troops with rifles firing the new cartridges, but equally they had do it as cheaply as possible. Moreover, such was the pace of invention that if they plunged into a particular system and adopted it, who was to say that a better system would not appear within a month or two? The obvious solution – and the one which had the most appeal – was to find a method of converting all the existing percussion muzzle-loading weapons as an interim measure, after which they could take their time about selecting the ultimate replacement. Most countries adopted similar solutions: take the existing percussion rifle, cutting away the chamber area and dropping in a new chamber that was hinged to the existing barrel.

An early example was the Snider conversion, invented by Joseph Snider of New York in 1866, and adopted by, among others, the British Army. The existing Enfield percussion rifle had the top of the breech end cut away, and the rear end of the barrel so exposed was formed into a chamber for a self-contained cartridge. Hinged to the side of the remains of the rear end was a block carrying a firing pin and an extractor claw. The block was lifted open and a .577 cartridge (consisting of an iron base with a cap in its centre and a cardboard and thin brass body holding a charge of powder and a bullet) inserted into the chamber. The hammer was cocked, the block closed, and the rifle fired. Opening the block again, the soldier jerked it backwards and the claw caught under the iron rim of the cartridge and pulled it far enough back for him to grasp it and throw it clear. The French Tabatiere conversion was very similar, as was one by Karel Krnka of Bohemia. The Americans adopted a system in which the block was hinged at its front end and lifted forwards to expose the chamber, but otherwise the principle was the same, and the Springfield "Trapdoor" conversion entered service in 1870, staying in use until replaced by a bolt action magazine rifle in 1892.

Gurkha soldiers of the Indian Army skirmishing in the 1870s, and using the Snider rifle, a breech-loading conversion from the Enfield muzzle loader.

Two countries which didn't need to worry unduly about conversions were Germany and France, for they both had serviceable bolt action rifles. However, these did not use metallic cartridges. The French were the first to move, still smarting from their defeat in 1871, and in May 1873 Capt Basile Gras of the French Army produced his conversion of the Chassepot to use a metallic center-fire cartridge. It was adopted in the following year in 11 mm (.43 inch) caliber and in 1876 by Greece.

Germany was in less of a hurry, having beaten the French in 1871, and when Nikolaus von Dreyse produced a conversion of his father's needle gun, the army turned it down, which left an opening for Mauser, one of the greatest names in firearms history.

Peter Paul Mauser (born 1838) and his brother Wilhelm (born 1834) were sons of a gunsmith in Oberndorf-am-Neckar, Germany. They both served their apprenticeships at the Royal Wurttemburg Firearms Factory, and in 1865 began work on improving the needle gun. They attempted to interest various government departments in their invention without much success, and then fell in with an American entrepreneur called Samuel Norris, who persuaded them to set up a workshop in Belgium and continue their work there. Patents were taken out jointly by the Mauser brothers and Norris, who was providing some financial assistance in the hope of being able to sell the Mauser invention to the French as a replacement for the Chassepot. The French were not interested, so Morris decided there was no future in the Mausers, withdrew his financial support in 1869 and allowed the patent to lapse. The Franco-Prussian War then intervened, and after it was over, the Mausers returned to Oberndorf and submitted their latest design to the Prussian Rifle Test Commission, where it was almost immediately accepted. The Gebruder Mauser & Cie company was formed to build the rifles, with Peter Paul attending to the manufacturing side while Wilhelm became the administrator and salesman.

Peter Paul Mauser (1838-1914), the founder of the company of that name and the inventor of numerous Mauser rifles and pistols.

The Mauser M1871 rifle was a bolt-action single-shot weapon firing an 11-mm bullet from a metallic cartridge case. Locking of the bolt was done by turning the handle down in front of a lug in the gun body. The firing pin was automatically withdrawn as the bolt was opened and cocked as the bolt was closed, and there was a safety catch on the rear end of the bolt. Well-designed and well-made, it was Mauser's proverbial "foot" in the military "door".

In the same year, 1871, the British made up their minds about the various competing designs of rifle, and to replace the Snider conversion they adopted the Martini-Henry in .45 (11.43 mm) caliber, using a center-fire cartridge devised by Col Boxer, Superintendent of the Royal Laboratory, Woolwich Arsenal, Britain's military ammunition factory. It was a peculiar case of spirally-wrapped brass foil with an iron base rim. As Boxer originally designed it, the cartridge was long and straight-sided, but it was soon found that this was not the ideal shape for the Martini action, since the cartridge had to be loaded across the top of the open breech block, and this meant either a short cartridge or one which could bend in the middle. Since the latter was out of the question, Boxer had to shorten the cartridge, but if he did that it would not be large enough to contain the quantity of gunpowder necessary to obtain the best from the rifle. So he invented the "bottle-necked" cartridge – one with a fat body which was narrowed down towards the mouth to fit the bullet. This gave the necessary capacity for the powder, but kept the cartridge short enough to be loaded across the curving top of the Martini breech.

In 1884 Mauser went back to the Test Commission with a new design – he had improved his 1871 rifle by simply adding a tubular magazine under the barrel and fitting a cartridge lifter operated by the movement of the bolt. Now the rifle could be loaded with eight rounds and fired as rapidly as the bolt could be operated – its service adoption placed the German Army comfortably ahead of its rivals in the field of small arms technology.

The French had also been looking at this question of a magazine rifle, and in 1886 they adopted a similar design – a bolt-action using a tubular magazine in the form of the Lebel rifle. But they also took another significant step and modified the ammunition. Until that time the accepted military rifle caliber was about .45 of an inch, or about 11 mm, using a heavy lead bullet. But the round invariably left traces of lead in the rifling, and after some time this built up into a serious impediment, and had to be scoured out with wire brushes and similar desperate measures. "Patching" the bullet by putting a paper sleeve around it slowed down the rate of lead fouling, but failed to do away with it. Similarly, the use of gunpowder had always introduced fouling into any firearm, and taken together with lead fouling, presented serious problems. But in 1885 a French chemist named Vielle had developed a nitro-cellulose explosive which could be used in place of gunpowder – it produced almost no fouling and very little smoke, and it also delivered a great deal more energy for a given weight of charge. The French realized that not only could they now reduce the size of the cartridge and still obtain the desired pressure, but also reduce the size of the bullet and still have sufficient striking energy to inflict lethal wounds.

In the early 1880s a Capt Edouard Rubin of the Swiss Army began looking at this business of lead fouling in rifle barrels. He determined that lead was necessary to give the bullet the weight and mass it needed to be effective, but by reducing the diameter of the bullet and putting a thin jacket of copper or steel around it, he finished up with a bullet which was just as effective, but which didn't leave any lead in the rifling. This became known as the "compound" bullet, and as Rubin's experiments became known, other countries began to look into this type of bullet.

And so in 1886 the French introduced the Lebel rifle in 8-mm (.315-inch) caliber, using smokeless powder and firing a lead-core, cupro-nickel jacketed compound bullet. Once again, they had pulled ahead of the race, opening up a fresh era of military rifle design as a result.

But there were other designers at work elsewhere, and they had different ideas. In Austria it was Ferdinand von Mannlicher who produced a design, adopted by the Austro-Hungarian Army in 1885, which introduced the concept of packet-loading or, as it came to be known, clip-loading. It also introduced another new idea in the form of the straight-pull bolt action, which meant that instead of lifting the bolt handle to unlock and then pulling it back to open, you simply grasped the handle and pulled it straight back. Pulling the handle of the Mannlicher bolt first lifted a wedge beneath the bolt out of engagement with the body of the rifle, and then drew the bolt backwards. This obviously provided a faster and smoother action than the awkward lifting through 90° and then pulling required by other bolt-actions, but it also made many soldiers mighty suspicious, since there didn't seem to be any obvious locking of the bolt, and they were fearful that the explosion of the cartridge might blow the bolt out backwards at the firer. It never happened with a Mannlicher bolt, but it certainly did happen with some other, less well-designed, systems, and the straight-pull bolt has never been as popular as might have been expected.

Drawings of the 8 mm Lebel rifle of 1886, the weapon which introduced smokeless powder, jacketed bullets of small caliber and the tubular magazine to the military world.

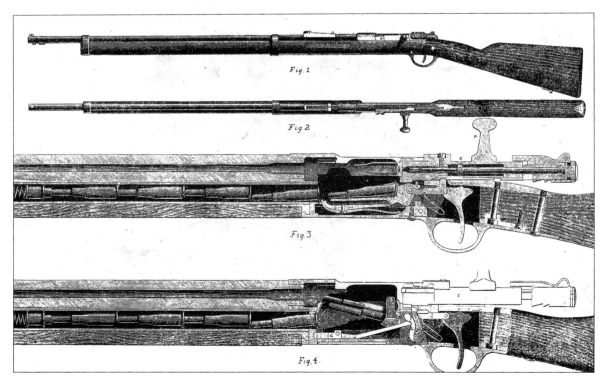

Fig. 1

Fig 2

Fig. 3

Fig. 4

But it was the packet-loading system which caught everybody's eye. Mannlicher put a box-shaped magazine underneath the bolt, and into it, after opening the bolt, the firer dropped a spring steel clip containing five cartridges. As he closed the bolt the lower edge struck the topmost cartridge, forced it out of the clip and into the chamber, and then the bolt locked. Beneath the clip was a spring-loaded arm which pressed on the bottom cartridge and forced the remaining four cartridges up in the clip. Therefore, after firing, when the bolt was opened and the empty case ejected, the return stroke of the bolt again caught the topmost cartridge and loaded it, and the spring-loaded arm pushed up the three remaining cartridges once more. This went on until the last cartridge had been loaded, whereupon the clip, now empty, dropped out of the magazine through a hole in the bottom. After the last round was fired and the bolt opened, another clip could be dropped in, and off the soldier went again.

Clip-loading was obviously a quicker and easier task than loading every cartridge singly into a tubular magazine, and so in 1888 the German Army abandoned the Mauser and adopted a new rifle designed by the Military Testing Commission at Spandau Arsenal in Berlin. This "Commission Rifle", like most things designed by committees, wasn't quite the perfect answer to all the problems, but it broke new ground. Firstly, it reduced the caliber to 7.92 mm (.311 inch); secondly, it introduced a rimless cartridge case which made feeding from a magazine easier since there was no protruding rim to catch on the round beneath; thirdly, it introduced a compound bullet; fourthly, it adopted von Mannlicher's clip-loading system; and fifthly, it took the Mauser bolt and added two locking lugs on the bolt head which locked into recesses in the chamber. Altogether, the Commission were convinced they had developed the ideal military rifle, and it was adopted by the German Army forthwith.

The clip-loading system, though, has one outstanding practical defect. If the soldier has fired, say, three rounds from his five-round clip, and there is a pause in the battle, he cannot "top up" his magazine to its full five rounds, nor can he load a single round into the chamber and keep his two rounds in reserve. A clip-loading rifle will only load a full clip, and once the clip is loaded, you cannot load a single round straight into the chamber over the top of the clip. This worried a number of soldiers, and caused Mauser to give the matter some thought. By the time the Belgian Army began casting around for a new rifle in late 1888, they stipulated that it had to have a packet-loading system which would also permit the loading of single rounds over a full magazine and would allow a half-empty magazine to be topped up with loose cartridges.

Mauser was ready with the answer. He had developed what we now call "charger loading", though many people refer to it as clip-loading. The difference is fundamental – in the new system Mauser used a thin metal clip which gripped the base of the cartridges, and a box magazine beneath

71

A British soldier of 1890 with the Lee-Metford .303 caliber magazine rifle.

the bolt. The bolt was opened and the clip of cartridges dropped into a slot in the rifle body which passed across the top of the bolt like a bridge. From this position the cartridges could be pressed down by the thumb and ran into the magazine, where they were held under spring pressure against a stop in the rifle body. As the soldier took his thumb away, after pushing in the cartridges, he also flipped the empty clip out of the way. As the bolt was closed, so it caught the base of the first cartridge and pushed it forwards until it cleared the restraining stop and then rose up and was pushed into the chamber. At any time the magazine could be topped up to its maximum of five rounds simply by dropping a loose round on top of the topmost cartridge and pushing it down against the spring until it caught under the stop. The soldier could also open the bolt and insert a loose cartridge on top of the full magazine whenever he so wished, pushing forward the bolt and loading the new cartridge without affecting the contents of the magazine. This was attractive to the military, since it meant that the soldier could keep up a steady fire, single-loading each round, until the enemy got close enough to charge, whereupon he had the full five rounds in his magazine for rapid fire.

The Belgians accepted this rifle, in 7.65 mm (.32 inch) caliber, as their Model 1889. Mauser had enough on his plate by this time manufacturing rifles for various countries, and Peter Paul was also having to do all the administrative work since his brother Wilhelm had died in 1882. An arrangement was therefore made whereby the Belgians would manufacture the rifles in their own country under license from Mauser. They set up a special consortium of manufacturers, and this became the *Fabrique Nationale d'Armes de Guerre*, which eventually became famous as simply FN.

During the 1880s the British had also been busy. In 1880/81 a selection of rifles had been tested, and one designed by James Paris Lee had emerged superior thanks to its reliability. Lee was a Scotsman who emigrated to the USA and entered the gun trade. He had developed a turning bolt rifle which sold in small numbers, and he then developed a box magazine which fitted beneath the bolt and could be removed so that an empty magazine could quickly be replaced with a full one. After some years of trials and changes, the British took to the Lee bolt and magazine and allied it to a new cartridge using a .303-inch (7.7-mm) compound bullet designed by Rubin, and propelled by a solid pellet of gunpowder. The barrel of the rifle was designed by William Metford – an English gunsmith with considerable expertise in designing rifling – and the final result therefore became known as the Lee-Metford rifle, issued in 1888. The magazine held eight rounds and the bolt had a single lug which turned into a recess in the gun body and a rib which locked in front of the "bridge" over the bolt.

With all these designs, and many more, appearing thick and fast, one thing you could be sure of was that each inventor was patenting his ideas as fast as he could think of them. This made life very difficult for designers appearing later in the field, for all the good ideas were already patented, or so it seemed. And since these designers wanted to make something of their ideas, they had to think hard so as to avoid copying somebody else's patent (thus having to pay royalties) and have something of their own to patent (and thus earn royalties). The trouble was that to get around existing patents often led to a complicated solution. Consider, for example, the Krag-Jorgensen rifle from Norway.

In 1887 the Danes, who had been using a single-shot Remington rifle, decided they needed a magazine rifle to keep up with the rest of Europe. After considering the Lee, they cast around locally and found, in Norway, a design which (though there is no cast-iron evidence) was probably cheaper and promised to be just as effective. Ole Krag was the Director of Kongsberg Arsenal and Erik Jorgensen the Works Superintendent, and between them, in the 1880s, they developed a rifle system. It was a turn-bolt, using only one locking lug and with a peculiar magazine which lay

A selection of breech-loading rifles of the 1870s; top left, the Soper-Henry, top right the Remington Rolling Block, and beneath are three pictures of the Martini-Henry action.

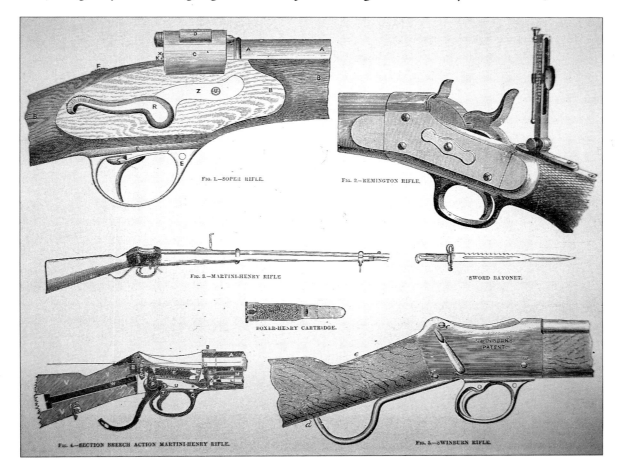

Fig. 1.—SOPER RIFLE.

Fig. 2.—REMINGTON RIFLE.

Fig. 3.—MARTINI-HENRY RIFLE.

SWORD BAYONET.

BOXER-HENRY CARTRIDGE.

Fig. 4.—SECTION BREECH ACTION MARTINI-HENRY RIFLE.

Fig. 5.—SWINBURN RIFLE.

horizontally across the rifle beneath the bolt. A trap-door on the right side of the rifle was opened and five cartridges pushed in, after which the trap was closed. This trap-door also carried a spring and "follower" which pressed against the loose cartridges and forced them across the rifle and then up the left side, until the first cartridge came to a slot alongside the bolt. Here a stop held the cartridge until the bolt was closed, when the bolt head caught the cartridge rim, forced it forward to clear the stop and then drove it into the chamber. The follower pushed on the remaining cartridges and the topmost cartridge took up its position ready for loading. Again, you could always top up the magazine by opening the trap and dropping in the necessary number of cartridges, and you could single-load if you wished. The Danes felt that this was just what they wanted and adopted it in 1889, the Norwegians following suit in 1894. However, what was more interesting was that the US Army, after testing some 50 different weapons, adopted the Krag in 1892, preferring it over the Mauser. Why? Because of one unique feature – you could top up the magazine of the Krag, as I have said, by simply opening the trap. Unlike any other rifle, you did not have to open the bolt. So if you were interrupted by some inconsiderate hostile while reloading, you simply dropped the cartridge, shouldered your rifle and fired, then went back to topping up.

Mauser spent the 1890s improving his design and selling rifles across the world, and in 1893 he sold a design to Spain which fairly represented his idea of perfection. It used a bolt with three locking lugs, two on the bolt head and one on the bolt body, a reinforced chamber for high-pressure cartridges, improvements in the extractor and firing pin and a charger-loading system which allowed the magazine to be topped up, and which concealed the magazine in the stock of the rifle, instead of in a protruding metal case. This weapon so impressed the German Army that they asked for a version in 7.92 mm caliber and, abandoning the Commission rifle, re-armed with the Mauser Gewehr 98 which, in a slightly modified form, was to serve them for the remainder of the bolt-action era.

There was one more major change to be made and one more major re-arming to be done before the bolt-action rifle settled down. During the Spanish-American War of 1898 the US forces, using the Krag-Jorgensen .30 rifle, were confronted with the Spanish using the 7-mm (.275-inch) Mauser. Both were fairly evenly matched, the Krag firing a 14.3-gm bullet at about 535 m/sec (1,755 ft/sec), giving 2045 Joules (J) energy, while the Mauser fired an 11.2-gm bullet at 680 m/sec (2,230 ft/sec) to give 2589 J, a difference which, considering that a mere 50 J is enough to knock a man down, isn't really significant. But at the Battle of San Juan Hill the Spaniards, well positioned in entrenchments, inflicted quite severe casualties on the attacking Americans. This should have occasioned no surprise, given the terrain and the fact that magazine rifles were in use, but the Americans came to the conclusion that the

A US Infantryman of the
Spanish-American War with
his .30 Krag- Jorgensen
rifle. A painting by
Frederick Remington.

Spanish Mauser rifle, and higher velocity cartridge, were the key features
and decided to seek a fresh design.

While they were thus employed, the British began fighting in South
Africa and soon began to question one of the long-standing customs of

the military rifle world. Ever since rifles had first appeared it had been the practice to develop two different models – a long-barreled infantry rifle for the ordinary infantry soldier, and a short-barreled carbine for use by cavalry, artillery, engineers and others who needed a rifle from time to time, but for whom it was not the primary weapon. In South Africa these people were frequently called upon to fight as infantry, and it appeared that there was little difference in the shooting, whatever weapon was in use. Was it really necessary to perpetuate the two (or more – the cavalry wouldn't deign to touch the engineer's carbine, and the artillery insisted on its own pattern) types of rifle? Apparently not, and when the time for a periodic review and improvement of the Lee-Enfield rifle (similar to the Lee-Metford, but with a new barrel designed at Enfield for smokeless powder), the "short rifle" was invented. Shorter than the "long" infantry rifle, longer than the carbine, the short rifle was far easier to manipulate in battle, was easily carried by cavalry and artillery and similar troops, and shot well enough for anybody. And so the Short, Magazine, Lee-Enfield came into use in 1903.

At the same time the Americans had picked up the same vibrations, and reached the same conclusions in their search for a new rifle to replace the Krag. Deciding that the Mauser bolt and magazine system was the best on offer, for $200,000 they acquired a manufacturing license from the German company, developed the rest of the rifle to suit their own preferences, adopting the "short rifle" policy, and in 1903 introduced the Springfield M1903, complete with a new .30 rimless and smokeless cartridge.

While the rifle experts were hard at work, the rest of the firearms industry was not standing still. In particular, the revolver had come of age. The Smith & Wesson master patent expired in 1869, and with that out of the way, everybody and his uncle began manufacturing cheap revolvers. Nowadays, these are lumped together as "Suicide Specials", simple single-action solid-framed revolvers in calibers from .22 to .44 and always of the cheapest possible construction to sell at the lowest possible price. But in addition to these, the reputable makers were also at work turning out weapons of far higher quality and, at the same time, making mechanical improvements almost every year.

Smith & Wesson were quick to make their mark by introducing their American model in 1870, which featured a hinged frame so that the revolver could be opened and a central extractor in the cylinder would force out the empty cartridge cases, leaving the empty cylinder exposed for reloading. It was the first large-caliber revolver (in .44 caliber) to be specifically designed for metallic center-fire cartridge, and this together with the simultaneous ejection, made it instantly popular. So popular that in 1870, when the Russian Army decided to equip its cavalry with a revolver, it was the Smith & Wesson (S&W) American that they selected –

except that they didn't think much of the accuracy and redesigned the cartridge to use a larger bullet so as to be a better fit in the bore. The improved weapon was startlingly accurate, and was immediately called the S&W Russian model – the contract called for 215,740 revolvers, and S&W spent the next five years turning them out on schedule, which didn't leave them much time for attending to the domestic market.

Which was unfortunate, because this was the period when the American West was opening up, and a reliable, large-caliber revolver was an essential part of every pioneer's outfit. And if S&W couldn't provide them, then Colt would – and did. Initially, they marketed a rimfire version of their open-top percussion revolver, but this didn't sell very well, and the US Army wouldn't look at it, so they set about a new design which proved to be a master-stroke. They produced the Single Action Army Model 1873, although few people called it that – instead, everybody knows it as the Frontier or the Peacemaker, or simply the Single Action. But, like the Luger and the Thompson sub-machine gun, it is an instantly recognizable weapon – the archetypal "cowboy's gun".

Technically speaking it was no great advance – a solid-frame pistol, it was loaded by opening a "gate" on the right side and slipping cartridges in one at a time while turning the cylinder. To eject the empty cases you opened the gate and pushed down an ejecting rod mounted under the barrel to punch out the cases one by one – a far cry from the simultaneous ejection of the S&W. But it was foolproof, and there was nothing that could possibly go wrong with it. A single-action hammer was cocked by the thumb and fired by the trigger, and that was that. If the mainspring broke, you could always hit the hammer with a rock to make it fire, while

The immortal Colt Single Action Army Model of 1873, also called the Peacemaker, the Frontier Model and "Colt's Equaliser".

COLT'S,
New Breech Loading
METALLIC CARTRIDGE REVOLVERS.
FOR SALE BY THE TRADE GENERALLY
—MANUFACTURED BY—
Colt's Patent Fire Arms Manufg. Co.,
HARTFORD, CONN.

COLT'S,
METALLIC CARTRIDGE,
Army Six Shot Revolving Pistol.

.44 Calibre, Weight 2 lbs. 11 oz., Weight of ball 212 grains or 33 to the pound.
The Drawing is one-half the size of the Pistol.
PRICE $16.

COLT'S,
METALLIC CARTRIDGE,
Navy Six Shot Revolving Pistol.
.36 Calibre, Weight 2 lbs. 11oz.. Weight of ball 140 grains or 50 to the pound.
The general appearance of the Pistol is the same as that of the Army Pistol. See cut above.
PRICE $15.

A rare advertisement for the first Colt breech-loading revolvers which appeared in 1871. They were the same open frame design as Colt's percussion revolvers but failed to sell, so Colt thought again and produced the Model of 1873.

if the trigger broke, you thumbed back the hammer and let it go, and it fired. It was, in sum, accurate, robust, reliable and inexpensive – about $15 in its plain and basic form – and that was exactly what was wanted in the mining camps, on the plains, in the mountains or basically anywhere in the wilds. The US Army adopted it, and it sold by the tens of thousand in all sorts of calibers, although principally in the .45 caliber version. It was to stay in production without a break until 1940, by which time 357,859 had been made.

Having got two good models, both S&W and Colt stayed with these basic patterns and developed a range of revolvers in various styles and calibers – the Colt models were always solid-framed gate-loading types, while the S&Ws were hinged-frame self-ejecting types, and both firms eventually abandoned the single-action mechanism and used double-action (except, of course, on the Colt 1873, which stayed a single-action all its life). Various other manufacturers also made revolvers more or less based on these two – Harrington & Richardson, for example, produced a range of cheap hinged-frame revolvers which, at a quick glance, are hard to distinguish from the contemporary Smith & Wesson models.

Next came the turn of Colt to innovate, and in 1889 they produced a new revolver in which the cylinder was carried on a hinged arm (the "crane") so that by releasing a catch it would swing out to the side of the revolver. An ejector rod in the center of the cylinder was now pushed back so that it forced out the empty cases, the revolver being quickly reloaded and the cylinder swung back into the frame. This was adopted by the US Navy and, in gratitude for this recognition, Colt called it the Navy Model 1889, and made it available in .38 and .41 calibers.

S&W produced their own version of the side-swinging cylinder in 1896 in the form of the .32 Hand Ejector model – the two guns differed in detail only. Broadly, the Colt was distinguishable by having the front end of the ejector rod unsupported, while the S&W system had their ejector rod anchored to a lug underneath the barrel. In both types the rear end of the ejector rod sprang into a recess in the frame behind the cylinder, and was released by a catch in order to open.

In the early 1900s a further refinement was added. Ever since the earliest revolvers there had always been the danger that if the weapon was accidentally dropped and landed on its hammer, this would be sufficient to drive the hammer in and fire the cartridge under it, to the distress of anybody in the neighborhood. Similarly, if you were cocking the hammer and your thumb slipped, the gun would go off, and you might not have actually wanted it to do so. In 1904 Colt fitted an additional arm to the firing mechanism which prevented the hammer falling far enough to hit the cartridge cap unless the trigger was properly pulled back. This Positive Safety Lock became an important sales feature, and existing revolver designs which had this added to them also got the word Positive added to their name, so that the .38 Police model now became the .38 Police Positive Model. In 1906 S&W followed Colt's lead with a "rebound slide" which did the same job of preventing the hammer falling unless the trigger was pressed, but did it in a different way.

The ultimate refinement of the side-opening cylinder revolver came in 1908 with S&W's First Model .44 Hand Ejector. It was the same general design of swing-open cylinder, but a third locking lug was added on the front of the crane, locking to the extractor rod casing – a device requiring some precision in manufacture. Instead of simply having a lug under the barrel, there was now a metal shroud, forged as part of the barrel unit, in which the ejector rod lay, and which contained the front lock. The

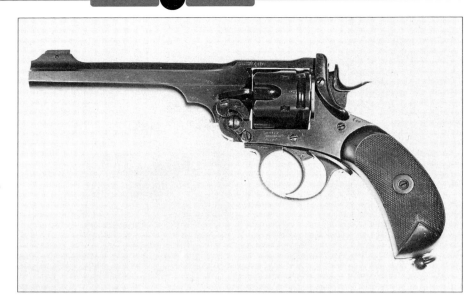

A Webley Mark IV British service revolver in .455 caliber; there were six different "Marks" of Webley revolver in all, but they all looked very much the same, hinged-frame auto-ejectors of immense strength.

revolver became known as the Triple Lock, and sometimes as the New Century or Gold Seal, from the gold medallions inlet into the grips. A beautiful weapon, it was made only until 1915, when wartime pressures made the triple lock too slow a manufacturing proposition, and about 20,000 were manufactured, a number of which were in .455 Webley caliber for the British Army.

The Webley was the other great military revolver. It armed the British and Commonwealth armies from 1887 to 1954, and is still in use in several countries today, even though the Webley company no longer manufactures revolvers. The basic design – a heavy, hinged-frame, six-shot, double-action pattern – changed very little over the six models accepted for military service. It was in .442 caliber at first, changing to .455 in the 1890s, and then changing again to .38 in the 1920s. Perhaps not quite so graceful as the American revolvers, it was, nevertheless, just as accurate, robust and reliable, and even when the Royal Small Arms Factory at Enfield decided to build the army's revolvers in the 1920s, they virtually pirated the Webley design to do it.

Webley are also worth remembering for their innovative Webley-Fosbery Automatic Revolver which appeared in 1901, and remained in production until 1915. It was the invention of Col Fosbery VC, and comprised the standard Webley revolver redesigned so that the cylinder and barrel unit could slide across the top of the butt frame. A zig-zag groove in the cylinder wall rode across a stud in the frame, so that when the pistol was fired, the recoil forced barrel and cylinder back, and the stud caused the cylinder to rotate one-twelfth of a complete turn. The hammer was also cocked on this rearward stroke. A return spring then drove the barrel unit back to the firing position, and as it moved, so the stud gave the cylinder another one-twelfth turn, so bringing the next loaded chamber in front of the hammer. It was an excellent weapon, loved by target shooters, but the exposed grooves and mechanism were defeated by the mud of the trenches of World War I, and Webley had such enormous orders for conventional revolvers that they abandoned production in 1915.

CHAPTER FIVE

FROM GATLING TO THOMPSON

THE IDEA OF A GUN which would emit a continuous stream of bullets, and thus overcome any number of enemy was one which had tempted inventors ever since the first weapon had been made, but, as we have seen, the mechanics of the flint and steel, powder and shot era were against it. The arrival of the percussion principle revived interest, and the American Civil War provided an incentive, which led to the Agar Coffee Mill gun, so called because the ammunition was fed into the top through a hopper resembling an old-time coffee-grinder. A number of steel tubes were provided with the gun, into each of which powder and a bullet were loaded – on the end of each tube was a nipple on to which a percussion cap was placed, and the tubes were then dropped into the hopper. A handle at the rear was turned; this pushed the first tube from the hopper into the chamber of the barrel, locked the breech block behind it and then dropped a hammer onto the cap and fired the bullet out of the barrel. Continued rotation of the handle withdrew the empty tube and ejected it, then fed the next tube in and so on. The gunner's mate had the job of picking up the empty tubes and reloading them as fast as he could, dropping them back into the hopper.

It worked, and, for its day, worked well, Agar claiming that he could fire 100 shots a minute. Experts claimed this was nonsense. "You propose to explode a pound or so of gunpowder every minute inside this gun. It will not withstand the heat." They had a point, but they would have been better employed trying to work out how to disperse the heat instead of rubbishing the whole idea. Agar, in spite of having a war around him, never sold more than about 50 guns.

The Gatling gun was widely adopted by navies as a means of combating fast torpedo boats and also, as shown here, for sweeping the decks of enemy ships by using guns mounted up in the rigging.

83

The Montigny
Mitrailleuse, with the
cartridge-holding plate
partly raised out of the
breech. Although
mechanically efficient, it
suffered from being
tactically misused during
the Franco-Prussian War
of 1870.

Instead, the "battery gun" became popular. This was no more than the 14th-century ribaudequin brought up to date – 24 rifle barrels mounted on a light cart, each loaded with a brass cartridge containing gunpowder and a bullet with a hole in the base. A steel block closed all 24 breeches and was perforated to allow the flash from a single cap to pass through and ignite the 24 cartridges in a ragged volley, after which the 24 barrels had to be emptied of their cases by hand and reloaded before the gun could fire again. But it produced a useful blast of fire which could cut down a charging enemy, and the Billingshurst-Requa Battery Gun became popular in the Civil War for protecting vulnerable points – notably bridges and similar places where an enemy attack would be channeled into a narrow space, ideal for such a weapon. As a result, these were often called "bridge guns".

In Belgium in the 1850s, a Capt Fafschamps had invented something similar but more efficient. He passed his ideas on to a man called Montigny, who turned them into a weapon known ever since as the Montigny Mitrailleuse. Montigny spent some years on his design, and was then able to interest Emperor Napoleon III of France – in 1869, in conditions of great secrecy, the French Army was equipped with 156 Mitrailleuse. It consisted of 25 rifle barrels mounted inside a tubular casing which resembled a cannon, mounted on a field gun carriage. At the rear end was a breech block containing 25 firing pins, which could be slid back, exposing the chambers of the rifle barrels. A plate holding 25 cartridges was then dropped into a slot in the face of the block, the latter being pushed forward and the cartridges entering the barrel chambers. Revolving a crank at the rear now caused the 25 firing pins to fall in succession, the rate of fire depending upon how fast you turned the crank – one quick spin would discharge all 25 barrels in one second. The block was then opened, the plate full of empty cases removed, a fresh plate dropped in, block closed, spin the crank and so on. A well-drilled crew with a supply of ready-loaded plates could keep up a rate of about 250 shots per minute.

Armed with the Mitrailleuse and the Chassepot rifle, the French went to war with Prussia in 1870 with high hopes, but the Mitrailleuse proved a disappointment. It worked well enough, and the Germans were respectful of its power, but the tactical handling of the weapon was entirely wrong. The French treated it as a form of artillery, deployed it in the open at long range, and thus invited the Prussian artillery to shoot it to pieces, which they did. It was very nearly the death-knell of the machine gun idea, but eventually it was recognized as a tactical mistake, and the gun was reprieved.

But the most famous of the "mechanical" machine guns is undoubtedly the Gatling Gun of 1861, the invention of Dr Richard Jordan Gatling. Although qualified as a dentist, Gatling never practiced, and spent his life inventing things – only the gun has perpetuated his name, his steam-plough, hemp-breaker and mechanical rice-planter all having vanished into history with his many other inventions.

Gatling more or less took the idea of the Agar gun and applied it to a conventional metallic cartridge. He also saw the point about the heating power of multiple explosions, and arranged for his gun to have six barrels which would be fired in turn. So that if the gun had a rate of fire of, say, 600 rounds per minute, any one barrel would only be firing at 100 rounds per minute, and would thus not get so hot. The six barrels were mounted on a central axis and behind them was the loading and firing arrangement, controlled by a revolving crank handle at the side of the gun. The cartridges were placed into a hopper above the gun and fed into the breech by gravity.

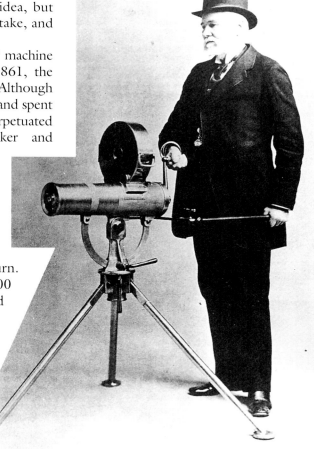

Dr. Richard Jordan Gatling demonstrating a lightweight Gatling gun which he recommended for use by US Police forces.

**The US Army Gatling
machine gun M1882 on
its standard field
carriage.**

As the handle was turned, the six barrels and the breech mechanism
revolved, each barrel having a bolt and a firing pin controlled by a shaped
groove in the casing around the breech. As the breech revolved, so the
bolts were opened and closed and the firing pin released by the action of
studs running in the groove. If we take one barrel as an example, when it
was at the topmost point of its revolution the breech bolt was fully open
and as it passed beneath the hopper so a cartridge dropped into the feedway. As the barrel continued to move round, the bolt was closed, leaving
the firing pin cocked, and as the barrel got to the bottom-most point, so
the firing pin was released and the barrel fired. Further revolution caused
the bolt to open and the empty case to be ejected, just in time for the
barrel to reach the top again with the bolt open, ready to collect its next
cartridge.

Gatling had a working gun in 1861, but apart from a handful bought
for test, and a dozen bought by Gen Ben Butler and used at Petersburg,
he met with little encouragement, largely because his sympathies were sus-
pected by both sides. It was not until 1866 that the US Army formally
adopted the Gatling gun, ordering 50 guns of 1-inch caliber and 50 of
0.50-inch caliber. In the 1870s the British gave the gun a comprehensive
test against the Mitrailleuse, a field gun firing shrapnel and a dozen rifle-
firing soldiers. The result was so conclusive that the Gatling was adopted
in .42 caliber for the army and .65 caliber for the Royal Navy.

At much the same time the Russian government, preparing for one of their periodic wars with Turkey, ordered 400 Gatling guns. Their Gen Gorloff was sent to the USA to oversee manufacture and inspect the guns before acceptance and shipping. With considerable cunning, he had name-plates prepared bearing his own name, which replaced the Gatling name-plates before the guns were finally sent off to Russia. This led to the following report appearing in the *Journal de St Petersburg* for 27 November 1870:

> The mitrailleuse adopted in Russia is a model invented by Maj-Gen Gorloff, and based upon the American Gatling system. The Gorloff gun, however, only resembles the Gatling in its exterior form, and is quite original. In perfecting his arm Dr Gatling has, it appears, been guilty of important plagiarisms on the Gorloff model, which has a just title to the name of the "Russian Mitrailleuse".

A fine early example of Russian propaganda.

There were other mechanical machine guns: the Gardner, which consisted of two barrels mounted side by side and their breeches opened and closed by a rotary crank; the Nordenfelt, with several barrels lying alongside each other and fed with cartridges by a back-and-forth movement of a lever; and the Lowell, which used a reciprocating breech block rather like that of the Gatling, and had three barrels, but only fired through one. Once that one was hot, the second barrel was rotated into position and firing began again, and when that was hot, the third barrel was used, and when that was hot the first barrel had cooled down and came into use again, and so on. This gun is recorded as having fired 50,000 rounds in two working days on test in 1875 with only two stoppages. It might have had a glorious future, but by the time it was perfected and ready to compete in the market-place, Hiram Maxim had appeared, and the idea of the mechanical machine gun was as good as dead.

Hiram Maxim was born in Sangerville, Maine, in 1840, and once of employable age, was apprenticed to a coachbuilder. After that he worked in a shipbuilding yard and a machine shop, giving him a wide-ranging knowledge which, allied to his amazing inventive ability, led him into the fields of electric lighting, gas generating plants, steam and vacuum pumps, engine governors and even a steam-driven airplane. According to a story he frequently told, he was attending the Electrical Exposition in Paris in 1881 when he met an acquaintance who told him "Hang your electricity! If you want to make your fortune, invent something that will allow these fool Europeans to kill each other quicker!" Whether this was true or just a good story, Maxim certainly went to London, hired a workshop in Hatton Garden, and set to work studying firearms. He soon put his finger on the one vital fact – that when a gun was fired, an enormous amount of energy was released, only a small portion of which actually drove the bullet. The rest went to waste, and so Maxim set about finding some way of putting it to use. Between 1882 and 1885 he studied and analyzed every possible way of using this energy, and patented every possible (and some impossible) way of operating a gun. Indeed, had he been so minded, he could probably have quoted one of his many patents and stifled machine gun development for the next 21 years, since almost every successful machine gun design can be foreseen in a Maxim patent.

He eventually came to the conclusion that the recoil energy of the weapon was the most reliable method of driving his gun, and in 1884 he demonstrated his first working model. It was chambered for the British Army .45 Martini-Henry cartridge, and was quite unlike any weapon which had ever been seen before. When the gun was ready to fire, with a cartridge in the chamber, the breech block was firmly held against the rear of the barrel by a large hook. When fired, barrel and breech recoiled in the gun body for about half an inch, after which the hook lifted, the barrel stopped moving and the breech block was free to continue its backwards movement, extracting the spent case. The block was attached to a connecting rod and flywheel crank, and as the block recoiled it drove the flywheel round about three-quarters of a complete rotation, so that the energy imparted to the flywheel caused it to drive the block back, feeding a fresh cartridge into the breech, forcing the barrel forward and allowing the hook to drop and lock the breech again. The flywheel stopped and the firing pin was released to fire the cartridge. The recoil from this shot now drove the flywheel in the opposite direction, once more completing the entire cycle of extraction, feeding and firing. Maxim adopted this system of alternate changes of direction so as to avoid the danger of a crank rotating always in the same direction, gradually accelerating and running away with itself.

Maxim demonstrated this gun before the Duke of Cambridge, Commander-in-Chief of the British Army, and his staff, and although it aroused some interest, they were non-committal – after all, the Duke was known to be against any change "until the time was ripe", and when asked when the time would be ripe, invariably answered "When change can no longer be avoided". So Maxim went away, re-examined his gun and, with the advice of some sympathetic army officers, set about making it simpler, lighter and more reliable.

He re-appeared in 1885 with his new design, which was entirely different to the first model. It still used recoil as the driving force, but had the cumbersome flywheel crank replaced by a toggle joint instead. An extension frame attached to the barrel carried the "lock", or breech-block, and behind it was an arm, hinged in the center and pinned to the lock at one end, and to a cross-shaft at the end of the extension at the other end. When the breech was closed, this hinged toggle lay flat and resisted opening. On recoil, the barrel and lock moved back together, keeping the breech securely closed until the bullet had left the barrel and the breech pressure had dropped to a

safe value. This took about half an inch of rearward movement, after which a crank on the end of the cross-shaft struck a fixed roller. This gave the cross-shaft a rotary motion which caused the rear link of the toggle to move downwards, so that the hinge in the middle of the toggle now allowed the lock to fly back and eject the spent case. As the cross-shaft turned, so it tensioned a spring, and after the lock had come to rest, the spring pulled the toggle up again and forced the lock forward to feed a new cartridge into the chamber. As the toggle came up into line, so it locked the breech, the gun fired, and the whole cycle started again. Ammunition was supplied by a cloth belt stitched into pockets, each pocket carrying a cartridge, and the movement of the lock extracted a cartridge from this belt, fed it down in front of the chamber, and moved the belt one cartridge at a time. So long as somebody kept the trigger pressed and the belt was long enough, the Maxim gun would fire forever, deriving its energy anew from every shot it fired.

Not surprisingly, Maxim soon came up against the heating problem foreseen in the Agar gun, and evaded so neatly in the Gatling, but with an automatic machine gun there was no way of slowing things down to allow the gun to run less hot. So he invented the idea of a water-jacket around the barrel, so that the heat of the barrel was passed into the water, and thus the barrel kept cool.

A demonstration of the second model of the Maxim gun in 1885; Hiram Maxim in the background, left. Note the smoke, due to using gunpowder cartridges.

89

Another Maxim demonstration, this time to Chinese envoys, at the Vickers-Maxim testing ground in Cumberland, England. How to chop a tree down without using an ax.

Maxim now toured Europe demonstrating his gun – he had to demonstrate it, because until people actually saw it firing they generally refused to believe that it was possible to fire ten shots every second. One story from this tour refers to the King of Denmark, who refused to have the gun in his army since "it would bankrupt the nation in ten minutes!" But sufficient people were impressed for Maxim to return to England and set up the Maxim Gun Company to begin production, supplying guns to Britain, Germany, Austria, Italy, Switzerland and Russia by 1890.

The success of the Maxim gun led other inventors to look into the possibilities of self-powered machine guns, and among the earliest of these was another notable American, John Moses Browning. Browning was already well-known for his designs of rifles and shotguns, and in 1889 he began working on a machine gun. Instead of using the recoil, he decided that the muzzle blast from the weapon was a useful source of energy if it could be tamed. His first test model used a perforated plate in front of the muzzle – the bullet went through the hole in the plate, but the spreading blast hit the plate and, via various levers and cranks, operated the breech to reload the gun and fire the next shot. This, though, was a clumsy arrangement, and his next move was to drill a hole in the barrel, just behind the muzzle. Beneath the barrel was a hinged arm, the tip of which lay beneath the hole, so that the emerging gas, part of that driving the bullet, forced the end of the arm down and, by levers, operated the breech. By 1890 he had perfected this design and offered it to the Colt company. They built a working gun, and this was adopted by the US Navy in 1895. The up and down action of the hinged arm led to these being christened the Colt "Potato-Digger" by the sailors. Browning is said to have encouraged Colt to put their name to the gun, because by the time they came to produce it, Browning had had a better idea and wanted his name to be remembered for the better gun, whenever it appeared. He got his wish, as we shall see.

In Europe, the first practical design appeared in Austro-Hungary. In 1888 the Archduke Karl Salvator and Count Dormus between them patented a very simple gun operating on the "blowback" system. There was a heavy breech-block and a powerful spring, and the block was never actually locked to the barrel. When the cartridge was fired the inertia of the heavy block and the power of the spring kept the breech closed just long enough to allow the bullet to leave the muzzle of the short barrel, and as the pressure dropped, so the block began to move, compressing the spring. After it had lost its energy, the spring returned it, loading the next round and firing it. Despite being both simple and reliable, the gun's lack of a breech lock meant that it could only use relatively weak cartridges. Nevertheless, the design was sold to the Skoda company, and as the Skoda machine gun, remained in service until 1919.

In 1893 another Austrian, Capt Odkolek, had an idea for a machine gun and decided to take it to the Hotchkiss company in France. Hotchkiss was

British naval ratings at machine gun practice with a Maxim in 1896; notice the small water jacket when compared with later models. These guns were for use by naval landing parties, the fore-runners of today's SEALs and Commandos.

91

THE STORY OF THE GUN

then being managed by American Laurence V. Benet, who was an astute businessman. He saw the germ of an idea in Odkolek's design, so he bought it, and although its inventor argued for a royalty deal, Benet refused, and offered him outright cash instead. Odkolek accepted, to his lifelong regret, because after Benet had finished with tidying-up his design, the result became the Hotchkiss machine gun, which was used all over the world.

The Hotchkiss was gas-operated, using some of the gas which was pushing the bullet through the barrel. This escaped through a port in the barrel and was directed into a cylinder beneath the barrel. There, it drove a piston back to unlock and withdraw the breech block, loading a spring as it did so – the spring then pushed the breech block and piston back, loading a fresh round. Ammunition was carried in a pressed metal strip which was fed into the side of the gun, and the movement of the breech also withdrew the cartridges from this strip and moved it across, until when it was empty it was pushed out on the other side of the gun. The gun was adopted by the French Army in 1897, and proved reasonably reliable, but it was prone to overheating in spite of having massive brass fins on the barrel to try and dissipate the heat. In 1900 it was replaced by a new model with steel fins, which improved things slightly, but it was not considered sufficient an improvement by the French Army, and they set out to upgrade it, without reference to the Hotchkiss company.

Their first attempt was by the arsenal at Puteaux, who produced the Model 1907 gun – this was more or less the 1900 Hotchkiss with a lot more brass fins on the barrel and a variable rate of fire device of dubious value. As a field service weapon it was a failure, and it was withdrawn and retained only for use in fixed fortifications.

A Model 1914 Hotchkiss machine gun, seen here protecting the French Settlement in Shanghai during the Sino-Japanese war in 1932. Note the ammunition feed strip sagging out of the side of the gun.

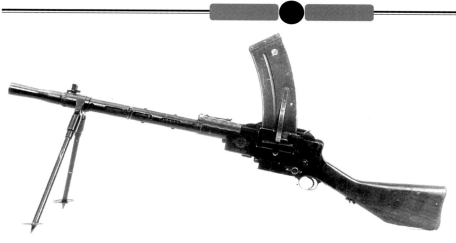

Next came the St Etienne arsenal with their Model 1907. This could best be described as a Hotchkiss with everything changed for the sake of changing it. It used a gas piston, but instead of blowing it backwards, blew it forwards, so that the direction of motion had to be changed by a gear system in order to move the breech block backwards. The gas cylinder had an adjustable volume so that the rate of fire could be altered, and several other ill-advised changes were made, but the remarkable thing was that it retained the Hotchkiss strip-feed system, which was the one thing most people considered to be the only serious defect of the original Hotchkiss design. The St Etienne guns appeared to perform reasonably well, but real use in 1914 soon exposed their many defects, and they were eventually given to the Foreign Legion while the army returned to the basic Hotchkiss design.

The Hotchkiss was also bought by Japan, and in 1904 they used it to good effect against the Russians in the Russo-Japanese War. The Russians were using the Maxim, and this was the first war between two major powers in which the machine gun saw extensive use. The Russians were the first to demonstrate their power at the Battle of the Yalu River, where eight guns beat off several Japanese attacks. The latter, using a lighter gun, were able to carry their Hotchkiss guns forward in their attacks to provide portable firepower, and this decided the result of the battle on several occasions.

The Russians also had another machine gun in use – a light weapon carried by their cavalry in the form of the Madsen, one of the most remarkable designs ever produced. It was the first gun which could be called a light machine gun – it was produced almost without change for over 50 years, and was used as an infantry weapon, a tank gun and as aircraft armament, all with equal success. Although used by over 30 countries, it was never officially adopted as the service machine gun by any one single power. And it was the most fiendishly complicated mechanism ever to achieve any sort of success – as an expert once said to me, "The amazing thing about the Madsen is not that it works well, but that it works at all!"

A Danish Madsen machine gun; although this is the Model of 1950, there is practically no difference between this and the 1904 models which armed the Russian cavalry.

93

Action in the Russo-Japanese War, 1904, the war which introduced machine guns, barbed wire, hand grenades and other armaments which were to make an even greater impact ten years later in World War I.

The Madsen began life as an automatic rifle, but it proved cumbersome and was abandoned for that role to become a light machine gun. Designed by a Dane called Schouboe, the gun was recoil-operated and was virtually an adaptation of the rising-block breech of the Martini rifle to an automatic action. When the round is fired, the block is aligned behind the barrel, and pins in the front end of the block are riding in grooves in the "switch plate", a track cut inside the gun body. As the barrel and bolt recoil, the pin on the breech block is drawn along the groove, and the angle of the groove causes the block to lift up, clear of the chamber. A separate extractor, driven by a cam on the barrel, extracts and ejects the cartridge case. As barrel and block continue moving back a hammer is cocked and a recoil spring compressed, after which the barrel and block stop moving. The spring now pushes them back again, and the breech block pin is switched into a lower groove so that the block is swung down, below the mouth of the chamber, allowing a rammer to ram a cartridge out of the overhead magazine and into the chamber. The rammer returns to rest, and just as the barrel arrives back at its firing position, the switch plate groove drives the breech block up to close the breech and the hammer then falls to fire the round. Thus, in distinction to every other machine gun, the bolt merely opens and closes. Everything else – extracting and reloading – is done by separate pieces of the mechanism, and yet it works quite reliably. It tends to balk a little with some rimmed cartridges, preferring rimless rounds, because the feed path is actually curved, but it has been produced in most of the world's popular calibers and would certainly not have survived so long had it been liable to frequent malfunctions.

By the mid-1900s, the Maxim gun had been around for some 20 years, and one or two people began to think it could stand an overhaul. That it was reliable and effective there was no argument, but it had been built in days when stress calculation was in its infancy, and nobody, anyway, knew what sort of stresses a machine gun might suffer. As a result, it was a good deal heavier and more massive than it needed to be. And in 1909, when the German Army began contemplating the application of aircraft to military tasks, it was felt that at some time in the future a lightweight machine gun might be needed on such machines. Since the government arsenal at Spandau, which built the German Maxims, was busy, the task was given to a commercial company, the *Deutsche Waffen und Munitionsfabrik* of Berlin. Their designer, Heinemann, spent two years on the project and in 1911 produced the Parabellum machine gun. By careful choice of materials, and some alterations in design, he saved some 35 lbs in weight – the water jacket was done away with, replaced by a perforated jacket which allowed air to flow past the barrel and cool it (bear in mind this was envisaged for fitment to a moving airplane) and there was a shoulder stock and pistol grip to allow the aircraft's observer to fire it conveniently. Mechanically, it was changed by having the toggle lock break upwards, instead of down as in the Maxim, a change which allowed the receiver to be somewhat smaller. The result was a very good weapon which, in due course, became a major aircraft armament. Had the army been sufficiently farsighted, it could also have been used as an excellent infantry light machine gun, but nobody thought of that in 1911.

The Maxim also underwent some changes in Britain, although there the object was mainly to make it easier to manufacture – nobody envisaged its use in an airplane either. The mechanical change involved was the same as that in the Parabellum (reverse the movement of the toggle so that it broke upwards), and careful choice of materials. and dimensions reduced the weight by 18 lbs. As the Vickers gun, it remained a tripod-mounted, water-cooled weapon, and it continued to serve, without further alteration, from 1912 until the 1960s.

When war broke out in 1914 the machine gun was generally held, in the British, French and German Armies, on a scale of two guns per infantry battalion. It is commonly believed that the Germans had far more than anybody else – one official American document claimed 50,000, which is ridiculous – but the truth is simply that their apparent superiority was due to stripping the guns from their reserve forces to thicken up those in the frontline. The British and French did not do this, and hence the apparent difference. One reason why the former didn't follow suit was simply that they had no reserve

A British instructor from the Machine Gun Corps introduces two members of the American Expeditionary Force to the Vickers machine gun in 1917.

machine guns worth speaking of – the development of the 1913 Enfield rifle, and the accompanying .276 caliber cartridge, caused the procurement of Vickers guns to be stopped once the initial orders for the Regular Army had been fulfilled. There was no point in making .303 machine guns if the service caliber was going to be changed in a couple of years – better to wait until .276 had been confirmed and then re-design the Vickers gun and put it into production. And since the .276 Enfield was stillborn, no more production of Vickers guns took place until after war had been declared.

The scale of machine guns was quite adequate for open warfare – which it had been designed for – but once the trench line was established, the demand for the weapon grew daily, and soon all the combatants were casting about for production facilities and, more importantly, for designs which were less expensive and easier to make than the Maxim derivatives. Another requirement which began to make its presence felt was the need for a lighter weapon which could be carried into an attack by one man – the three-man team needed for the Maxim and Vickers class of gun, due to its weight and cumbersome mounting and belts of ammunition, was not a convenient method of taking a machine gun forward, and not a system which allowed it to be brought rapidly into action during an attack.

In the USA, an inventor called Samuel MacLean, and his companion Col O. M. Lissak, had begun the design of a gas-operated light machine gun in about 1907. They had attempted to interest the US Army in the weapon, with no success, and eventually, in disgust, sold the design and patents to the Automatic Arms Company and retired from the firearms development field entirely. The Automatic Arms people looked around for somebody who could take this undeveloped design and turn it into a workable•gun, and in 1910 they approached Col Isaac Newton Lewis of the US Army. Lewis was a coast artilleryman, at that time Director of the Coast Artillery School at Fortress Monroe, and he had developed a number of fire control devices for artillery use. He accepted the challenge and in 1911 had five working guns which he demonstrated to the US Secretary of War, the Chief of Staff and other senior figures, after which he handed over four guns to the Board of Ordnance. What happened after that was an astonishing example of clashing personalities.

At that time the Chief of Ordnance for the US Army was Gen Crozier, an autocratic man who believed that only the Ordnance Department knew anything about weapons – and that any weapon for the Army had to be developed by Ordnance personnel in an Ordnance establishment. Moreover, he resented the fact that Lewis had worked on this gun while being a serving officer in the US Army (in spite of the fact that Crozier was receiving royalties for a gun carriage he had designed several years before). So only over Crozier's dead body would the gun ever get into US Army service. Lewis soon saw which way the wind was blowing, took back his four guns, resigned "on the grounds of ill-health", took himself off to Belgium, and once there, set up a company called *Armes Automatique Lewis* to make the gun. In fact, what Lewis did was license manufacture to BSA (Birmingham Small Arms Company) in Britain. And when war broke out very shortly afterwards, the entire production capacity of BSA went into making Lewis machine guns for the Belgian Army, then for the British and Italian Armies. Their production was not sufficient, and the Savage Arms Company of Utica, New York, was given a contract, and by 1917 were turning out 400 guns a week.

The Lewis gun, as it was now known, was an excellent weapon. It was gas-operated and had a toothed rack on the piston which wound up a clock-type spring when driven back by the propellant gas, after which the spring propelled it back again. A pillar on the end of the piston fitted into a helical slot in the bolt, so that as the piston moved back it first rotated the bolt and then opened it, and on the return stroke it closed the bolt and then rotated it to lock, and finally the pillar struck the firing pin and fired the cartridge. Feed was from a 47-round drum which fitted onto a post on top of the gun body. The barrel was surrounded by a fat tubular jacket covering a number of aluminium fins, and as the gun fired so the muzzle blast drew air forward, sucking it in at the back end of this jacket, passing it over the fins to cool the barrel, and finally ejecting it at the front. It was just what the infantry needed as a one-man automatic weapon – it took about one-fifth of the time and materials required for a Vickers gun, and it allowed the firepower to be carried along in the assault, not left behind to fire overhead from a distance. But its greatest application undoubtedly came in the air.

THE STORY OF THE GUN

As early as June 1912 Col Lewis had persuaded the Commanding Officer of the Army Experimental Flying Station at College Park, outside Washington D.C., to take a Lewis gun up in a Wright biplane and fire it at a ground target, using a white cloth six feet by seven feet, and firing from 250 ft altitude. Several hits were achieved, and Capt Chandler, the gunner, fired the remainder of the drum into a pond to observe the fall of shot. Next day he tried again, from 550 ft, and got 14 hits on the cloth, but the army was not impressed. "Nonsense", they said. "Who would ever want to fire a machine gun from an airplane?"

Nothing daunted, Lewis persuaded the Belgians to try the same experiment in December 1912, and the British in November 1913. Again, nothing official ever came of it. But on 22 August 1914 two British aviators, Lts Strange and Penn-Gaskell, took a Lewis gun up in their BE.2C and took a few pot shots at a German Albatros at 5,000 ft. They reported what they had done, but it was rapidly pointed out to them that this was a "dashed unsporting attitude and should not be repeated. After all, the Germans might start shooting back, and then where will we all be?"

And, of course, sooner or later the Germans did start shooting back and the carriage of pistols, then rifles and shotguns, and finally machine guns became common practice. The Lewis was ideal for this role – in the first machines it was the observer's task to protect his pilot, and he had the Lewis mounted on a pillar alongside his cockpit, since it was light and

An early example of aircraft armament is this Lewis gun on a Belgian airplane in 1914. The mounting appears to be made from gas-pipe, and the observer would have to stand up in the cockpit to operate it, taking care not to shoot off his wing support pylon and wires or his propeller.

easy to swing around and he had room to store spare drums. Pretty soon it was found that a 47-round drum didn't last long, so a 97-round model was produced. When single-seat scouts came along the pilots wanted a gun with which they could attack other scouts, but the problem lay in the spinning propeller in front of the machine. The solution was to fit the Lewis gun on top of the upper wing of a biplane, usually on a curved rail which allowed the pilot to pull the gun back so as to be able to change the magazine. Sometimes pilots didn't bother and simply stood up in the cockpit to make the change, this being quicker than sliding the gun back and forth. There is at least one fully-authenticated report of a pilot (Lt Louis Strange again) doing this and losing control of his Martinsyde scout – it looped, leaving him hanging from the handle of the Lewis gun drum as the plane inverted, and dropped him back into the cockpit as it came right side up once more. If nothing else, this was a tribute to the robustness of the Lewis gun, and its magazine attachment.

One feature of the Lewis gun in the aircraft role was that the complex air-cooling system was regarded as surplus to requirements – the airflow over an aircraft doing 100 miles per hour would be quite sufficient to keep the gun cool – and so the radiator was abandoned and the bare barrel and gas cylinder allowed to appear, saving some weight in the process.

The French also adopted the Lewis for aircraft use, placing it on the upper wing of their Nieuport scout machines so as to fire above the propeller arc. But Roland Garros – a pre-war record-breaking aviator, and one of their more aggressive scout pilots – wanted to get the gun down on top of the engine where he could see across it and take a better aim, and after applying some thought to the matter he attached steel plates to the propeller at the point where each blade passed in front of the gun now mounted above the engine cowling. He then took to the air, pointed himself at a German machine and pressed the trigger. Some of the bullets hit the steel plates and ricocheted who knows where, but enough of them got through the space between the revolving blades to hit the German and shoot him down. Garros went on to become one of the foremost French "ace" fighter pilots.

His phenomenal success stunned the German pilots, who were mystified by his tactics, until he was shot down by flak in April 1915, and the secret of his steel plates was revealed – Garros was made prisoner, escaped in February 1918, went back to flying, but was shot down again, this time fatally, on 5 October 1918. The Germans now began to apply some scientific thought to this problem of firing through the propeller, and Dutchman Anthony Fokker – their principal aircraft designer – soon produced a mechanical synchronizer which permitted the gun to fire only when the propeller arc was clear. This was applied to a pair of Parabellum machine guns mounted alongside the engine, and the Germans soon had control of the skies over the Western Front.

The Allies were not far behind them, however, with the Constantinesco hydraulic synchronizer allowing a pair of Vickers guns to be mounted on British and French aircraft. Vickers guns were preferable to Lewis because they were belt fed, and thus avoided the business of changing magazines in the middle of a battle. Since the Hotchkiss machine gun used rigid steel strips for feeding the ammunition – an inconvenient system for the over-worked pilot of a single-seat fighter – the French adopted the Vickers as well.

In 1914, as the war broke out in Europe, the US Army was not partic-ularly well-provided with machine guns. The Colt "Potato-Diggers" had been relegated to the training role by this time, and the service weapon was the .30 Maxim Model of 1904, of which the army owned 282. Shortly after adopting this, the question of a light weapon for use by cav-alry arose, and a Hotchkiss design was adopted, known in American ser-vice as the Benet-Mercie Machine Rifle M1909. Springfield Armory man-ufactured 670 guns for the army and then a further 400 for the navy, hav-ing obtained a licence from Hotchkiss. The Maxim gun was well enough received and performed admirably, manned by trained machine-gunner specialists, but the Benet-Mercie suffered from being called a "Machine Rifle" – it was thought that trained machine-gunners were wasted on this device, and simple soldiers could pick it up as they went along, but the 1916 Mexican border troubles soon showed the defects in this system. The men had little or no training, and the gun was ineffectually handled, but at least the army recognized the trouble and thereafter took time to train soldiers in the handling and mechanism of machine guns, whether or not they were specialists – a system which was to pay them dividends in the next two years.

When the USA was pitchforked into the war in April 1917, and the army suddenly began to expand, the demand for every kind of weapon far outstripped the available supply, and factories were turned over to war production almost overnight. Machine guns were high on the list, and this had been foreseen – in 1915, it had been decided to adopt the British Vickers gun, converting it to fire the US .30 cartridge, and Colt were given a contract to produce several thousand guns. Production did not begin until July 1917, but thereafter the flow increased, and by the end of the war 3,125 had been made in the USA and another 6,112 obtained from Vickers in Britain.

In 1901 John Browning had begun working on a design for a recoil-operated machine gun, but at that time the army were not interested, and he put it to one side. He brought it out again in 1910, worked on it some more, found the army were still not interested and shelved it once more. By late 1916 it was fairly obvious that America would eventually get involved in the war, and Browning brought out his designs again, finished it off, demonstrated it to the army in February 1917, and submitted it for official trial in May. The performance of the gun was so impressive – it fired 40,000 shots without a single component breaking and with only two stoppages, both of which were due to the ammunition – that it was ordered into production without further ado as the Browning M1917 machine gun.

The M1917, like the Maxim and Vickers, was a water-cooled, belt-fed gun deriving its power from the recoil force. The mechanism, though, was entirely different. The barrel was attached to a trough-like barrel extension in which the bolt sat – behind this was the "lock frame", another trough-like piece into which the bolt could pass. On firing, the bolt and barrel recoiled back together, the bolt being locked into the extension by a vertical plate. After a short movement the plate was driven down and released the bolt, and at the same time the barrel extension struck two curved arms, called the "accelerator", on the lock frame. The tips of these two arms were driven back and struck the bottom of the bolt, giving it an additional boost backwards to compress a spring. During this movement the cartridge case was extracted and ejected, and the next round was drawn out of the feed belt. The round was then forced down into a slot in the face of the bolt until it was aligned with the chamber, by which time the bolt had stopped and now returned, ramming the fresh round into the breech. As the mechanism returned to the forward position, so the bolt lock plate was lifted to lock the breech securely in time to fire the next round.

All this may sound complicated, but as these things go, the Browning is a very simple mechanism – the outstanding feature is the invention of the accelerator, which gives the bolt a momentum which it would not otherwise achieve with a recoil stroke of only 15 mm. It allows the length of the gun's receiver to be less than would be required if the recoil force was unaided, because in that case the recoil distance would need to be larger. And a simple mechanism is easy to understand, easy to strip and assemble, and has a lot less to go wrong with it. As a result, the Browning machine gun, in a variety of forms and calibers, has been in service ever since 1917, and will probably reach its centenary without too much trouble.

The water-cooled ground gun was soon joined by an air-cooled version for use in aircraft and tanks, and in the early 1920s the air-cooled model was tried as a ground gun. The first attempt was not particularly successful, but a second version, with a short barrel, was then developed for use by the cavalry. This was better, but eventually the barrel length was restored to the original figure and, after a variety of test models had been tried out, the design was finally settled and the air-cooled M1919A4 model became the new infantry standard in about 1935 – it was intended to replace all the M1917 water-cooled guns, but in fact the M1917s continued in use until the middle 1950s before they were entirely replaced. The M1919A4 has now been retired from the US Army, but there are quite a few thousand still in use in other armies around the world.

The .30 caliber Browning M1919A4 machine gun, standardized in 1935 and still in wide use all over the world, many having been converted to the 7.62 mm NATO caliber.

One of the things to which John Browning turned his hand while his machine gun design was languishing was a lighter, and more portable, machine gun design. He visualized a heavy automatic rifle, magazine fed, and capable of being carried and used by one man. But he could see that in the 1900s the US Army had neither the money nor the tactical need for such a weapon, and he steadfastly refused to offer any military design outside the USA, so beyond sketching out his design he did little about it. But once things began to look serious he got the drawings out and set to work, offering it for test early in 1917. After testing the prototypes the army accepted it, calling it the Browning Automatic Rifle M1918 – even though it went into production in 1917, the M1918 title was chosen so as to avoid confusion with the M1917 Browning machine gun.

The Browning Automatic Rifle (or BAR, as it is always known) was a gas-operated, magazine-fed rifle in .30 caliber which could be fired either automatic or in single shots. The official policy was to use it for single shots as routine, keeping automatic fire for emergencies. In 1917 the Americans were besieged with French experts of every shape and size, and one of the suggestions which came from this source was that of "marching fire", in which the troops clambered out of their trenches and advanced towards the enemy carrying automatic weapons at the hip. These they fired constantly as they advanced, thus ensuring that the enemy kept his head down and didn't fire back at them. In theory, excellent – in practice not so good, because it fails to take account of the need to carry a fairly large supply of filled magazines, and the need to keep stopping and changing these magazines during the advance. But no matter, it was a good idea and the Browning Automatic Rifle fitted it perfectly – by the end of the war over 50,000 BARs had been made, and about half of them went to the AEF in France. Once tried, of course, the "marching fire" idea was soon seen to be mistaken, and it was quietly forgotten – the BAR, however, lived on to become the "base of fire" for the infantry section, an automatic weapon which the section could use to cover their advance in the same way as a machine gun when necessary, and which could simply function as a rifle at other times.

The BAR turned out to be another long-lived weapon, for after the war it was licensed to FN in Belgium, who sold it as a light machine gun to several continental armies and manufacture continued in the USA. It served through World War II and the Korean War with the US Army, largely because no suitable light machine gun had been developed which could replace it, but it eventually went out of service in the 1960s.

Back in France in 1917, the BAR was a desirable property but, of course, production was slow to get under way and meanwhile the US troops were desperate for a light machine gun. "No problem", said their allies the French. "We have an excellent model in production. *Voilà*, the Chauchat machine gun!" The American purchasing commission, I regret to say, fell for it and bought no less than 12,800 of the wretched guns, after which things got worse.

Browning M1919A4 machine guns in use in the Mekong Delta, Vietnam, in the 1960s.

The infamous Chauchat (or Chauchard, or CSRG), this being the French version in 8-mm Lebel caliber and with a semi-circular box magazine. The American version used the .30 Springfield cartridge and had a rectangular box magazine.

If there is one thing which the history of firearms tells us, it is that good guns get designed by designers, not by committees, and the Chauchat amply confirms this view. It was developed hurriedly in 1915 to satisfy the French Army's insistent demands for more machine guns. A four-man committee under Col Chauchat designed the gun and it went into mass-production. The basic design was sound enough, if unusual – it used the long recoil system of operation in which barrel and bolt, locked together, recoiled until they were well behind the magazine. The bolt was then unlocked and the barrel allowed to return forward to the firing position, after which the bolt was released to run forward, chamber a fresh round and fire. But if the design was sound, the manufacture was slipshod, the gun being made from stamped or turned parts so that it could be made in any engineering shop. Moreover, the peculiar 8-mm French cartridge, with a steeply tapering bottle-necked case with a large rim, demanded a peculiar semi-circular magazine which clipped beneath the gun. The manufacturing tolerances were large, much hand-fitting had to be done on each gun to make it work, and interchangeability of parts was impossible. It was unusual for any Chauchat gun to fire off more than two or three bursts without jamming, and due to the enclosed design, rectifying a jam meant dismantling the gun.

The American Army in France soon realized they had a problem, but it was thought that most of the trouble came from the 8-mm cartridge, and that if it could be adapted to fire the US .30 cartridge, and given a simple straight box magazine, things might be better. The French were approached and were agreeable, and the purchasing commission contracted for a further 19,200 guns in .30 caliber. The French accepted, with the stipulation that French inspectors would examine the guns and, if they passed them, the American Army would accept them without further ado.

The result was even worse than the original gun. The .30 round was much more powerful than the 8-mm Lebel, and the action of the gun became more violent, usually tearing the rims off the cartridges during extraction and producing even more jams. As soon as the BAR appeared the Chauchats were relegated to training use, and as soon as the war was over the entire stock was withdrawn and scrapped, apart from a handful left in museums. Yet the French continued to use it and, after the war, managed to sell it to various unsuspecting armies. It turned up again in the Spanish Civil War, and the reports of some members of the International Brigades indicate that it hadn't improved since 1918. The French still had some in store in 1939, and when the German Army occupied France the following year, they took one glance at them, and quickly offloaded the Chauchats onto auxiliaries and foreign contingents. And according to one source a number even appeared in the hands of the Viet Cong in the 1960s! Like the proverbial bad penny, the Chauchat will continue to turn up in spite of every soldier who ever sees one trying to get rid of it.

This question of providing the American infantryman with "marching fire" produced another solution in 1917 when a designer at the Remington Arms Company named J. D. Pedersen (whom we shall meet again) offered a rather unusual device to the US Army. It was a Springfield rifle converted into a form of machine gun by inserting a special bolt and breech assembly in place of the rifle's normal bolt. This insert contained a chamber and a blowback bolt and return spring, a firing pin and a magazine housing, all within the dimensions of the original rifle bolt, so that replacement was simply a matter of taking the Springfield bolt out and inserting the Pedersen Device. It fired a special .30 caliber pistol cartridge through the rifle's barrel, and ejected its empty case to the left of the gun through a slot which had to be cut into the wall of the rifle's receiver.

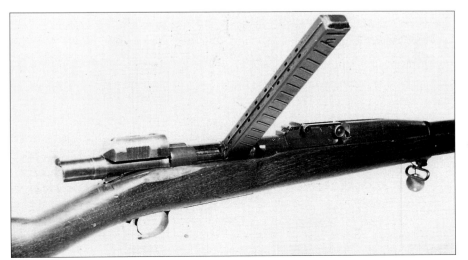

The Pederson Device, or Automatic Pistol Cal .30 M1918. A Springfield rifle with the bolt removed and what amounted to a sub-machine gun mechanism inserted in its place. The magazine stuck out obliquely from the top of the action. Never used in action, this model remained secret for thirty years.

Although the bullet was small and the velocity low – about 1,300 ft/sec – it was considered lethal out to 500 yards, and it was envisaged as being issued to every soldier, together with ten 40-round magazines. The soldier, when required to attack, would remove his rifle bolt, slip in the Pedersen Device, put a magazine on, and then clamber out of his trench and advance, spraying bullets as fast as he could operate the trigger, changing magazines as he went, and finally arriving at the enemy trench unscathed.

The whole device was kept highly secret – it was officially called the "Automatic Pistol, Cal .30, M1918" in order to conceal its true identity, and an officer was sent to France to show it to Gen Pershing. 100,000 devices were ordered and manufacture commenced, while the Springfield rifle production was interrupted and re-tooled to cut the ejection slot in the receiver. The order was later increased to 500,000, and of this some 65,000 had been made when the Armistice brought everything to a halt. In the calmer postwar atmosphere, the Pedersen Device was re-examined and the army came to the conclusion that it wasn't quite such a good idea after all. In the first place, the soldier could easily lose the bolt of his rifle during his traversing of No-Man's land; secondly, ten 40-round magazines placed a fairly heavy additional load on the soldier; and thirdly, the low-velocity near-misses failed to make as much of an impression on the enemy as did a high-velocity rifle bullet whipping past his ear. The verdict went against it and almost every one of the 65,000 were scrapped in conditions of complete secrecy; so secret that very few people ever knew it existed until well after World War II.

The 1914–18 conflict became a war of firepower – the two sides on the Western Front were locked into two lines of entrenchments, and any advance had to be simply a matter of overwhelming the other side with firepower so as to open a gap for the attackers to march through. On the Eastern Front it was more fluid, but there were strategic points where the Russians were well-entrenched and the same conditions applied. The best military minds on both sides applied themselves to the problem and two German officers on the staff of von Hindenburg on the Eastern Front came up with a new tactic. Gen von Hutier, an infantryman, and Col Bruchmuller, an artilleryman, developed a combined tactic in which the artillery, instead of pounding away at the frontline trenches and wire for days before an attack, thus alerting the enemy and wrecking the landscape, but doing little else, would drop sudden bombardments of gas, high explosive and smoke on to selected points in the enemy lines. Communications centers, supply dumps, artillery positions, machine gun posts, trenches – all would be dosed in turn at irregular intervals, some with gas, others explosive, and then on their next dose the medicine would change, so that nobody knew when they would be bombarded next, nor did they know what the bombardment would deliver. A short time of this is enough to make anybody jumpy.

At the same time, and concealed in the smoke and gas clouds and the general fog of war and confusion, small selected squads of highly-trained infantry would sneak across No-Man's land, probing for weak spots, filtering past obstacles and generally not looking to fight, but rather to act as guides for the mass of infantry which could follow as soon as these Storm Troops had pioneered a route. So far so good, but what von Hutier now asked for was some sort of highly-portable machine gun with which he could arm his Storm Troops so that they had the maximum short-range firepower should they run into any opposition. Nothing too heavy or cumbersome – the Storm Troops had to be highly mobile, and not be slowed down by excess weight.

As is often the case, the answer was there already, unrecognized. In early 1916 Hugo Schmeisser, chief designer for the Bergmann company of Berlin, had developed what he called a Musquete as a light and handy weapon for trench warfare and patrols. It was a simple blowback gun with a short barrel surrounded by a perforated jacket which could be gripped by the firer, a wooden butt and half-stock under the tubular receiver, and a side-mounted magazine housing into which the 32-shot "snail" magazine of the Luger pistol could be fitted by an adapter. Inside the receiver was a heavy bolt, a firing pin and a large spring. A slot in the receiver allowed a cocking handle on the bolt to protrude, and a notch at the rear end of the slot allowed this handle to be turned into it to prevent the bolt going forward, and so act as a safety device. To fire, the soldier simply pulled back the cocking handle until it locked behind the trigger sear. He then pulled the trigger, which released the bolt to go forward, collect a 9-mm Parabellum cartridge from the magazine, ram it into the chamber and stop, whereupon the loose firing pin in the bolt carried on forward and struck

The original sub-machine gun: the Bergmann MP18 in 9-mm caliber with the original Luger pistol "snail" type magazine.

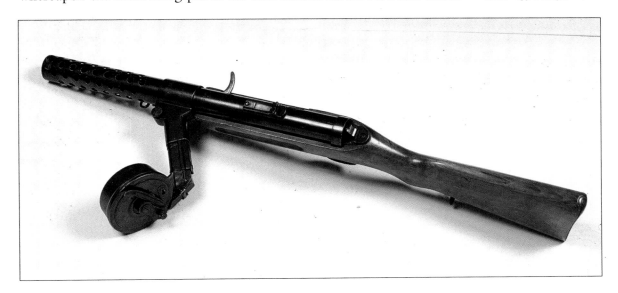

the cap to fire the cartridge. The pressure inside the cartridge blew the bullet up the barrel and also pushed back on the bolt, but since the bolt was a good deal heavier than the bullet, the latter was out of the muzzle before the impulse delivered by the cartridge case could get the bolt moving. So that by the time the bolt did move and pulled the cartridge case out of the chamber, the pressure in the chamber was down to a safe level – the case was ejected and the bolt went back and caught on the sear again, or not, if the soldier still had his finger on the trigger, in which case the bolt went forward and fired the next round. In fact, and although the term was not yet coined, Bergmann had invented the sub-machine gun.

Bergmann appears to have made a small number of these weapons and submitted them to the German Army for their opinion – they appear to have sent them to the front for some views from the troops. I say "appear" because there is little written evidence, though a British document describing the interrogation of a German prisoner-of-war in the latter part of 1916 has a very recognizable description of the Bergmann Musquete as having been issued for test to his company. But nothing further was done – doubtless the German Army thought it was quite a reasonable weapon, but didn't do much that other weapons couldn't already do, so there was no need to complicate the supply line.

In September 1917 the firm of von Hutier & Bruchmuller demonstrated the efficiency of their new combination of artillery fire and Storm Troops by capturing Riga in 24 hours, overcoming a defensive position which had defied attack for three years – at the time the victory was credited to von Hindenburg and his "Hindenburg Taktik", but the truth soon leaked out. Stock in the company rose, and they were invited to move across to the Western Front to apply their technique to the French and British trenches, at which point von Hutier raised the question of a light and portable weapon, and somebody remembered that thing that Bergmann had offered. It was tried, approved, and went into production as the Maschinen Pistole 18 (MP18), some 30,000 being produced before the war ended. And von Hutier and Bruchmuller did break the Allied line in April 1918, but the Allies managed to recover, regain the initiative, and end the war.

There is another contender for the title of the world's first sub-machine gun – an Italian weapon called the Vilar-Perosa. It too was a simple blowback weapon firing a 9-mm Parabellum cartridge, but its claim is invalidated by the tactical use to which it was put. Briefly, the Italian Army was principally engaged with the Austrians in the mountains which formed most of their joint border, and as a result they were constantly looking for lighter weapons which could be more easily carried up and down mountains. Long range was not necessary, since all engagements were close combat up there in the snow and ice, and in the latter part of 1915 the Vilar-Perosa was offered as a short-range support machine gun.

A twin gun was fitted to a tray-like carrier which the machine-gunner strapped around his neck like a match-seller, so that he could walk or climb and still have his twin machine gun ready for instant use. It failed to work in practice – can you imaging trying to clamber up an ice-bound mountain with a tray of machine guns slung around your neck? It was eventually withdrawn. The two guns were separated and a single gun was fitted to a wooden stock to become the OVP, or the Beretta M1918, according to who did the conversion. In this role they do qualify as sub-machine guns, but by that time the Bergmann had entered service.

The name "sub-machine gun" did not appear until after the war had ended, and was coined by American Gen John T. Thompson. A class of 1882 graduate from West Point, he first served as an artilleryman, then transferred to the US Ordnance Department in 1890. Thompson had a hand in the development of the Springfield M1903 rifle, did some famous tests on corpses and beef cattle to determine that the .45 bullet was the optimum performer for a handgun, and played a large part in the perfection and adoption of the Colt M1911 pistol. In November 1914 he retired, intending to devote his time to perfecting an automatic rifle, and joined Remington as their Chief Engineer. When the war broke out he became responsible for setting up a factory to manufacture the .303 Enfield rifle for the British, then another to make the 7.62 mm Mosin-Nagant rifle for the Russians, and when the USA entered the war, he was recalled to service and given the job of converting the Enfield rifle to .300 caliber, and organizing its manufacture. He was promoted to Brigadier-General and awarded the Distinguished Service Medal for his efforts in all these affairs, and for keeping the AEF in France supplied with weapons and ammunition. In December 1918 he retired for the second time.

During all this time, though, he had been keeping an eye on his automatic rifle development, and one of the things which had caused a problem in its early days was the choice of an operating system. Gas operation, he thought, would be too complicated for a shoulder arm, recoil operation would probably produce too heavy a weapon and blowback was out of the question with a powerful military cartridge. He was also anxious to find some system untouched by any major manufacturer so as to avoid payment of royalties on an existing patent. In 1915 he found a patent which had been taken out by a Cdr Blish of the US Navy – without going into too much abstruse detail, it can best be described as a method in which a slanting wedge held the breech block closed. The angle of the slant was critical, because it was calculated so that under high pressure, as when the cartridge exploded and forced the cartridge case back against the bolt, the wedge would jam in place and lock – but when the pressure dropped the wedge was free to move and would slip out and allow the breech to open. Thompson thought that this would suit his design very nicely, and he and Blish, with a financial backer called Thomas F. Ryan, formed the Auto-Ordnance

British troops in 1939 with Thompson sub-machine guns. Patrols along the Franco/German front discovered that the ammunition in the drum magazines slapped back and forth inside and advertised their presence; after 1940 the box magazine became the standard.

Company to develop the rifle. Two designer/engineers, Payne and Eickhoff, were hired, and when Thompson and Blish went back into service due to the war, these two continued experimenting.

They soon found out that the Blish system didn't work with the .30 rifle cartridge, but that it worked very well with the .45 pistol cartridge. When they passed this news to Thompson, he told them to forget the rifle and develop a hand-held machine gun which he called the Trench Broom, since it would sweep the trenches clear of the enemy. The war ended, Thompson and Blish came back, and in 1919 the Trench Broom made its appearance. By then, of course, there were no trenches to be swept, so Thompson, in a moment of inspiration, called it the Sub-Machine Gun and began promoting it as a police weapon.

There was some precedent for such employment, as the Allies had forbidden the German Army to keep the Bergmann MP18, but had approved its use by the German police, which says a good deal about the turmoil on the German streets in 1920! There was certainly little or no civil unrest in the USA, but on the other hand there was Prohibition, and with it the rise of the gangster and what we now call "organized crime". In fact, the actual number of Thompsons sold to police forces and used in the fight against crime was not all that high, but the gun caught the eye of the newspaper reporters and, as the Tommy-Gun, gained a high degree of notoriety – once Hollywood began making gangster movies, the Tommy-Gun was hardly off the screen. The name stuck, so much that the Auto-Ordnance company actually registered it as a trade-mark, though their principal concern was to stop anybody else using it rather than use it themselves.

In fact Auto-Ordnance had contracted with Colt for the manufacture and supply of enough parts to make 15,000 guns, with the Lyman company to make 15,000 sights and with Remington to make 15,000 stocks and grips. These components were all shipped to Auto-Ordnance who then assembled and marked them. Every now and then some slight improvement or modification would occur, and the marking on the gun changed accordingly from the M1921 to the M1928 by degrees, but basically every Thompson which appeared between 1920 and 1940 came from that stock of 15,000 sets of parts.

More publicity came with the discovery of a plot by the Irish Republican Army to buy 495 guns through a "front" man in New York and ship them across to Ireland, but no military notice was taken of the weapon until, in 1926, there was a particularly audacious robbery of a US Mail truck in New Jersey. The US Post Office asked for protection, and were given the services of the US Marines who, for this duty, were provided with 250 Thompson guns (paid for by the Post Office). A few weeks later, when the Marines were sent to Nicaragua to help the newly-elected President Diaz, they took the Thompsons with them – there is no record of what the Postmaster thought about his guns going to Nicaragua! In the following year, more Thompsons were acquired by the Marines for their detachment in Shanghai, and after reports on these weapons had been digested, it was formally approved for service as the Thompson sub-machine gun M1928.

A German policeman in the early 1920s carrying the Bergmann MP18 sub-machine gun; forbidden to the army by the Versailles Treaty, they were permitted for use by police forces.

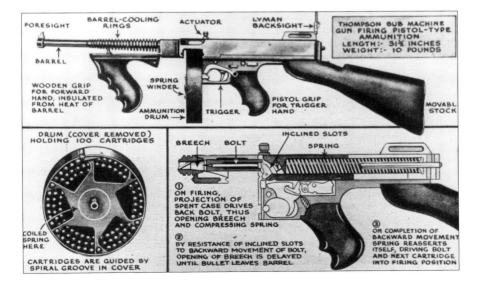

A page from a British Home Guard handbook showing the principal features of the Thompson sub-machine gun.

WANTED FOR MURDER
GEORGE KELLY alias "MACHINE GUN" KELLY

By his authority,
the Attorney General of the State
of Indiana offers a reward of

$3000.00

for information leading to the
capture of George Kelly.

DESCRIPTION
Age: 35
Height: 5-9
Weight: 185
Hair: brown
Eyes: brown
Complexion: light

CRIMINAL RECORD
Arrested Kansas City, Mo. '32, armed robbery.

Arrested Joplin, Mo. '32, attempted extortion.

Arrested Johnson City, Ka., bank holdup and shooting
of law officer.

THIS MAN IS HEAVILY ARMED AND DANGEROUS.
HE WAS LAST SEEN IN COMPANY WITH JOHN
DILLINGER AND OTHERS OF HIS GANG.

Unfortunately, the Thompson gun acquired a poor reputation in the 1930s, due to people like "Machine Gun" Kelly, Al Capone, Bonnie & Clyde and other criminals.

The M1928 is more or less the "definitive" Thompson, because one or two minor wrinkles had been ironed out by that time, and the gun was as perfect as it was ever going to get. It consisted of a square-section receiver, inside which was the bolt with a slot running down each side, sloping forward. Into this slot dropped the heart of the Blish system, which was the H-Piece, so-called because it looked a little like a metal "H", with the two lower legs in the bolt slots and the cross-piece in a slot in the top. The two upper legs were very short and served to couple the bolt to the actuator – a sliding plate with the cocking handle which protruded through a slot in the top of the receiver. There were also two sloping slots in the sides of the receiver, but sloping at a slightly different angle to those in the bolt, and the sides of the H-Piece had studs which fitted into these slots.

Now, with the bolt forward the H-Piece was engaged in both the bolt slots and the receiver slots. Pulling on the cocking lever caused the actuator to force up the H-Piece until it disengaged from the receiver slots, after which the pull was transferred to the bolt and the bolt was drawn back. Pressing the trigger released the bolt, which went forward and loaded a round into the chamber. As it did so, the H-Piece dropped into the receiver slots again. The firing pin went forward, the round fired, and the base of the cartridge case forced the bolt back. This high pressure caused the H-Piece to jam tightly in its slots, so locking the bolt. After the bullet left the muzzle and the chamber pressure dropped, this jamming effect was released and under the lesser pressure the H-Piece was forced to slide upwards in the two slots until the lugs came clear of the receiver slot and the bolt could be blown backwards. In fact, there had always been a dispute as to whether this really constituted a locked breech, or whether the Thompson was really a delayed blowback weapon. Whatever it was, it worked.

Ammunition was carried either in a 50-round drum magazine or a 20- or 30-round box magazine – indeed, various magazines were made and offered, but the 50 drum and 20 box were the most usual types. On the muzzle went the "Cutts Compensator", a cylindrical fitting with slots in the top which diverted some of the muzzle blast upwards and thus forced the muzzle down against the natural tendency of the gun to rise up when firing at automatic.

Anyone who has ever used a Thompson will agree that it was accurate, strong, and utterly reliable – stoppages were rare. It is notable that during World War II almost every specialist raiding force – Commandos, Rangers, Special Air Service and so forth – invariably selected the Thompson as their sub-machine gun. The unfortunate thing is that Gen Thompson, after nursing his "baby" through the years of The Depression, died in June 1940, and thus never saw the enormous expansion of production which was to come.

CHAPTER SIX

INNOVATIONS

ONCE HIRAM MAXIM had shown that it was possible to make an automatic weapon which would reload from the power generated by firing the first shot, a lot of inventors began to wonder whether the principle could be applied to other types of weapon, to pistols, rifles and even shotguns.

In the middle 1880s many pistol-minded inventors were taken with the idea of applying the bolt action of a rifle to a pistol – some merely produced manually operated bolt action pistols, but these were never very popular except with a few target shooters. Those who wanted a pistol wanted a repeating weapon, and therefore bought a revolver, and so inventors began trying to apply some repeating mechanism to the bolt action. For some strange reason almost all of this development took place in central Europe, and almost all took the same form – a weapon of much the same shape as a revolver, but with an operating arm which ended in a ring or loop ahead of the trigger. Placing one finger in the loop and pushing the lever forward caused a bolt to be rotated to unlock and then be withdrawn. A magazine, in the place occupied by the cylinder of a revolver, presented a cartridge in front of the bolt, and by then pulling the lever back again with the finger the bolt was closed, loading the cartridge into the chamber. The final movement of the operating arm either caused the trigger to be pressed, releasing a firing pin in the bolt, or at least brought the operating finger into close proximity to the trigger.

These "mechanical repeating" pistols worked well when they were new, well lubricated, and provided with clean ammunition. But once they were dirty, dry, or provided with ammunition which was not quite to the correct dimensions, they became stiff and difficult to operate. As a result they were never wildly popular, and are relatively scarce today. They might have been perfected, but their life was short – by the late 1890s they had been completely swept away by the rise of the automatic pistol.

One of the most familiar of war pictures, German troops invading Russia in 1941. The principal figure carries a Luger pistol and a stick grenade and is draped with an ammunition belt for the MG34 machine gun. The man behind is pointing a Mauser rifle. But at what?

But it was one of the mechanical repeaters which begat the first automatic pistol. An Austrian named Laumann had developed a typical bolt-action repeating pistol in 1890 – he then made some improvements, took out another patent, then completely revamped the mechanism and in 1892 patented an automatic pistol. For many years, based upon a Provisional Specification Laumann had filed, it was believed that the pistol was operated by the primer cap expanding backwards and operating a linkage, but in the 1980s a careful examination of his Final Specification showed that Laumann's design was a delayed blowback pistol. A "blowback" pistol is one in which the bolt and barrel are not locked together at the instant of firing, and only the weight of the bolt and the power of the spring behind it prevent the bolt from being blown open when the cartridge explodes. In fact, the weight of the bullet is so small compared to that of the bolt that it accelerates out of the barrel and the gas pressure inside drops, before the inertia of the bolt is overcome by the impulse given to it by the base of the cartridge case being driven backwards by the explosion. In a "delayed blowback" additional insurance is taken out by arranging a lever or some other device which slows down or otherwise hinders the opening of the bolt for a little bit longer. Laumann's pistol used a long lever which had to be forced back by the bolt, and by arranging the pivot of the lever at some distance from the bolt, a mechanical disadvantage was obtained which provided the requisite delay.

Laumann took his design to the *Oesterreichisches Waffenfabrik* at Steyr, in Austria, where it was produced as the Schonberger pistol in 8-mm caliber. Who Schonberger was has never been satisfactorily answered – some say he was the Works Superintendent at Steyr, others that he was Laumann's financial backer. No matter – the pistol was made and put on sale in 1893 or 1894. It didn't sell in any great numbers, but there is no doubt that it was the first automatic pistol to be offered commercially.

Next came a German called Borchardt. He had worked in the USA for Winchester and helped Sharps design a rifle, been foreman for the Singer Sewing Machine company, then returned to Europe in 1882 to work with Rudolf Frommer, a gun designer in Budapest. After a brief return to the USA in 1890, he appears next in Berlin in 1892 with the design of an automatic pistol, which he offered to Ludwig Loewe, a prominent firearms manufacturer. It is generally assumed that during his time with Frommer in Budapest, Borchardt had seen a demonstration of the Maxim gun and studied its mechanism, because his pistol used the same sort of hinged-in-the-middle toggle to hold the breech-block closed while the cartridge was fired.

The Borchardt pistol broke more new ground than had the Schonberger, because it was designed from the outset as an automatic weapon, rather than being a made-over mechanical repeater. It used a rimless 7.63 mm cartridge specially designed for it, and it carried a box magazine in the butt which fed the cartridges straight up to the face of the breech-block. The barrel had an extension at the rear end in which the breech-block slid back and forth, and behind the breech-block lay the toggle, pinned to the rear end of the extension and attached to a coiled spring in a circular casing below the rear of the pistol's frame. When the cartridge fired, the barrel and extension slid back in the pistol frame – after a short movement the toggle was broken by striking a curved ramp on the frame and the central hinge lifted, drawing back the breech-block and extracting the empty case. The rear section of the toggle pulled on the coiled spring and wound it up. Then the spring pulled back, down went the toggle, the block went forward to load the next round, the toggle straightened out and locked, and the pistol was ready to fire the next shot, a firing pin in the breech-block having been cocked.

Loewe put the pistol on the market in 1894 and some 3,000 were made and sold before production ended in 1899 – it was more of a commercial success than the Schonberger had been, and much of that was due to the better ammunition and better design. But with the best will in the world, it has to be admitted that the Borchardt was a cumbersome pistol – 11 inches long and weighing 41 ounces empty, it had an enormous overhang behind the butt, to which a lightweight wooden stock could be screwed to turn the pistol into a species of carbine. A few customers complained about the awkward handling, and Loewe probably suggested to Borchardt the he might try a redesign, but Borchardt appears to have been one of those people who, once they have got a design out of their system, don't wish to return to it, but go on to something else. Whatever the reason, Borchardt was reluctant to make any changes to his pistol.

Now it was Mauser's turn. He had seen the reception accorded the Borchardt, and it was obvious that the automatic pistol was the coming thing. As it happened, three of his employees – the brothers Federle – had been working quietly away on an automatic pistol for some time, and now Mauser invited them to work on it full-time, and they completed their first prototype in March 1895. Patents were immediately taken out in Mauser's name – a recognized commercial practice, as when employees developed ideas in the company's time, they then became the company's property.

One of the remarkable things about the Mauser C/96 pistol, as the Federle design came to be known, is that the production models differ only slightly from the prototype – they got it right first time, except for some fine-tuning, and the design never had to be seriously changed throughout its life. The pistol is recoil-operated, the barrel (and a barrel extension behind it) sliding on top of the frame which contains a box magazine ahead of the trigger – the most recognizable identification feature of the Mauser. A bolt slides back and forth in the barrel extension and carries a firing pin. Behind the extension, on the rear of the frame, is a

Wilhelm Mauser, brother of Peter Paul and the administrator and salesman of the partnership until his death in 1882.

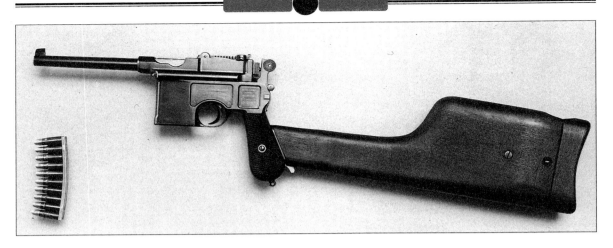

substantial hammer. At the instant of firing the bolt is locked to the barrel by a locking arm, attached to the barrel extension, which is forced upwards by a cam inside the frame and engages with the bolt. On firing, barrel and bolt recoil backwards for a short distance until the locking arm rides off the cam and drops free, unlocking the bolt. Barrel and extension then stop, but the bolt continues backwards, extracts the empty case, compresses a spring and cocks the hammer, then is driven forwards again by the spring, collects a round from the magazine and loads it into the chamber. The barrel and extension then move forward, the locking arm rides up the cam and locks the bolt and the pistol is ready to fire the next shot. It is a precise and strong mechanism, and one of the unique features is that there are no pins or screws in it – every part fitting into the others like a jigsaw puzzle.

The cartridge was adapted from the 7.63 mm Borchardt design, Mauser giving it somewhat more powder and altering some of the dimensions very slightly. It is a powerful cartridge, and advantage was later taken of this by making the holster of wood, with a tongue which fits into a groove in the butt of the pistol so that the holster becomes a wooden shoulder-stock, and the pistol can then be fired from the shoulder with reasonable accuracy to a range of about 200 yards.

The Mauser pistol went into production in 1896, and rapidly became popular. This relegated the Borchardt to a poor second place, and Loewe's *Deutsche Waffen-und-Munitionsfabrik* urged Borchardt to revamp his pistol to compete with Mauser, who looked very likely to walk off with a fat military contract to supply the German Army, such time as that body decided to adopt an automatic pistol. The experts still argue over who was responsible for what, but the fact remains that the working principle of the Borchardt pistol was taken as the starting point by Georg Luger, another employee of Loewe's, from which he developed the Luger pistol. This used the Borchardt toggle, but completely reorganized the design of the pistol so as to make it more handy, lighter and more reliable. The grip was raked back to an angle which matched the normal angle of the hand, so that aiming became almost instinctive (very few pistols have attained this perfect balance between the grip and the axis of the bore as did the Luger), and the cumbersome spiral spring and its casing was replaced by a leaf spring set in the rear edge of the grip and frame. Luger also realized that the 7.63-mm Borchardt and Mauser cartridges were too long and too powerful for his design, so he shortened the case and slightly reduced the charge to produce a 7.63-mm cartridge which has been known ever since as the Parabellum. The pistol, too, is properly called by the same name, even though it is universally recognized as the Luger – Parabellum was the telegraphic address of DWM Berlin, Loewe's company, and several of their products used it as a trademark.

Luger began submitting his pistol to various military authorities and testing boards, and soon found that, in general, they were not impressed with the 7.63-mm bullet. At that time most armies with any field experience had gained it against savage native tribesmen which were unlikely to be upset by being hit with anything less than a .45 lead bullet, and as a result most armies set .45 (or 11 mm) as the minimum caliber. Luger countered by developing a half-conical, flat-tipped bullet which, he claimed, improved the "stopping power" (the ability to stop an enemy in his tracks) to something approximating a .45 bullet. The Swiss believed him, tested the pistol, found it good, and in 1900 formally adopted it as the Swiss Army's official pistol. Luger had his foot in the door.

One of several types of Luger, this is properly known as the "Long '08" model, though it is frequently called the "Artillery" model. With a long barrel and fitted with a wooden stock, it doubled as a useful light carbine.

His next task was to convince the German forces, but they still balked at the 7.63-mm bullet. The cartridge was bottle-necked, to provide a short case with sufficient space for the powder, so Luger opened out the mouth of the case to the same diameter as the rest of the body, fitted a 9-mm bullet of the same flat-tipped, conoidal shape, and offered this to the German Navy. "That", they said, "was more like it", and adopted the 9-mm Luger in 1904 – the cartridge, of course, became the 9-mm Parabellum. This was enough to make the army take a second look, and in 1908 they adopted the 9-mm Luger as the Pistole 08.

So far, all the development of automatic pistols had been in Europe, but although there had been no production, work had been going on in the USA behind the scenes. John Browning had begun looking at the possibility of an automatic pistol as soon as he heard what was happening across the Atlantic, and in 1895 he turned up at the Colt factory with a design which used a similar mechanism to his gas-operated machine gun – a hinged arm on top of the barrel which was blown up by gas pressure and thus drove the breech-block. He signed a contract giving Colt the American production rights, and then had another thought – his design was in .38 caliber, and he had intended to sell the European rights separately, but he then realized that the largest potential market in Europe lay in the personal defense area, since armies would not consider anything less than .45 caliber. So he drew up another design, starting with the development of a new .32 caliber cartridge, and then going on to construct an entirely fresh pistol using blow-back operation. He patented this in 1897, and took it to Colt, but they could see little future in pocket automatics and declined his offer. As it happened, a representative of *Fabrique Nationale*, the Belgian factory set up to make Mauser rifles, was visiting the USA to study bicycle manufacture, since the factory in Liège was coming to the end of its rifle contract and needed work. He met Browning and took a sample of his new pistol back to Liège where, after testing it, the company decided to put it into production. Browning signed an agreement in 1897, although it was not until 1902 that he actually visited Belgium.

FN took a year-and-a-half to set up production, and the first pistols were made in January 1899 – about 4,000 were built, after which manufacture stopped, a few minor changes were made, and the new Model 1900 began production. In July 1900 FN had their first major success when the Belgian Army adopted it as their official sidearm, and issued a contract for 20,000 pistols. It remained in production until 1911, some 724,000 being made. No sooner was the Model 1900 on sale than Browning sat down to improve it, and a simpler design, the Model 1903, was the result.

The Model 1903 was based on a new cartridge, the 9-mm Browning Long. Browning realized that the .32 caliber was unlikely to attract much military support, even though the Belgians had bought it, and therefore developed a 9-mm cartridge which was suitable for use with a blowback pistol. Most contemporary 9-mm cartridges were too powerful to avoid the use of a locked breech, but by reducing the power, Browning could simplify the design of the pistol, and the Model 1903 was one of the simplest designs ever seen – and one which more or less settled the shape of the automatic pistol throughout the 20th century.

The pistol consisted of a frame, with the butt, trigger mechanism, a hammer and the magazine. The barrel was surrounded by a return spring, and an enveloping "slide" which slid back and forth on top of the frame. The barrel was attached to the frame by lugs under the chamber end, and the return spring was trapped by the end of the slide, which had a hole through which the muzzle appeared. By grasping the slide and pulling it back, this spring was compressed, and when the slide was released it was forced back to its forward position. As it did so the edge of the rear portion of the slide, which acted as a breech-block, loaded the topmost cartridge from the magazine. The hammer was concealed by the slide, and when the trigger was pressed it fell forward to strike a firing pin in the block portion of the slide. The pressure in the cartridge case blew the bullet out of the muzzle, and also forced the slide backwards to reload and recock.

The 1903 was an instant success, being purchased as a military pistol by several countries – in fact one of them, Sweden, still uses it. By January 1914 FN were celebrating the manufacture of their one millionth Browning pistol. But, at the same time, the simplicity of the design meant that it was pirated and copied in many places – it virtually founded the fortunes of a number of Spanish companies, because due to the peculiar Spanish patent laws of the time, it could be copied, since it was not officially on sale in Spain.

The Browning Model 1903 pistol, probably the most copied design in history. Millions have been made, licensed and pirated, and they are still in wide use all over the world.

Browning left FN with the rights to sell his pistols in Europe and the Eastern hemisphere generally. He then went back to Colt, pointed out the success his designs were having in Europe, and invited them to think again. They did, and accepted the 1903 pattern, making it in .32 caliber as the Hammerless Pocket Model, their sales area being the Western hemisphere, after which Browning retired to his drawing board and concentrated on a military design.

He had already submitted a locked breech pistol to Colt, who had begun work on it in 1899, and which was marketed as the Model 1900, a handful being taken by the US Army and Navy for trials. It used a similar frame and slide layout to the 1903 model, but the barrel was attached to the frame by two swinging links, one at the muzzle and one at the breech end – on top of the barrel were two upstanding lugs, and in the top of the frame were two matching grooves. With the pistol loaded and ready to fire, the barrel was tight against the top of the slide, lugs fitting into grooves, and the two links were almost vertical. A return spring lay in the frame, below the barrel, and was connected to the slide by a cross-pin. On firing, the slide was forced back by the power of the explosion, and because of the lugs and grooves, took the barrel with it, so that barrel and breech block were securely locked together for an instant as the bullet left the barrel. Then the continued rearward movement of the barrel caused the links to hinge backward, so bringing their upper ends down towards the frame and carrying the barrel with them, until the lugs came free from the slide grooves.

At that point the barrel stopped moving but the slide continued backwards to cock the external hammer and eject the spent cartridge case. The spring then drove the slide forward again, forcing a fresh cartridge into the breech, and then as it continued pushing on the base of the cartridge, caused the barrel to swing upwards on the links and bring the lugs back into engagement with the grooves.

The pistol worked fairly well, though it was complicated to dismantle for cleaning, and a number were sold commercially. Minor improvements were made, and then in 1905 the US Army decided that a .45 pistol was desirable (they had reverted to using .38 revolvers but had found them insufficiently powerful during the Philippine Insurrection), and Colt developed a .45 rimless cartridge and a new pistol to go with it. It was to the same design as the 1902, but it had no safety device and the army were, understandably, reluctant to accept it.

Browning then went back and made some changes to his design. He did away with the front link on the barrel and relied simply upon the front end of the slide to keep the muzzle end in the right place – now a single link beneath the chamber simply lowered the rear end of the barrel, the muzzle pivoting in a bush in the front of the slide, until the lugs came free. In theory, because the barrel begins to tilt before the bullet has left the muzzle, it should be less accurate than the parallel linkage, but in practice it made no measurable difference. He added a safety catch and also a "grip safety", a metal strip in the rear of the butt which had to be pressed in by the firing hand in order to allow the trigger and hammer to function. The US Army tested it thoroughly, accepted the design, and issued it as the M1911 pistol – following minor modifications in the 1920s as a result of experience during World War I, it was to serve until the 1980s as the official US military sidearm, and is still in production for commercial sale.

World War I set the seal of approval on the automatic pistol, although many armies were still loath to accept them in place of revolvers, and even before 1914, some designers were beginning to turn to the military rifle as the next field for development of the automatic principle. In fact, both Maxim and Browning began their experimenting by altering existing rifles to automatic action, but these were more in the nature of workshop models to prove a mechanical principle, rather than being practical weapons. As early as 1886 von Mannlicher had begun experimenting with various types of automatic rifle, and he produced a number of working prototypes, but they were delicate and complicated weapons, unsuitable for manufacturing in quantity. In the 1900s came designs from Mauser, Rigotti, von Mannlicher and Ross, to mention only the well-known names – there were a score of others now forgotten. And yet the first automatic rifle to see any serious production was from an entirely unknown name – Gen Manuel Mondragon of the Mexican Army.

Mondragon had patented his rifle in 1907, but there was nobody in Mexico capable of making it, and no manufacturer in the USA would listen to him, so he went to Switzerland and got the *Schweizerische Industrie Gesellschaft* (better known today by its initials SIG) to make the rifles for him. The rifle was gas-operated, using a piston to drive the bolt operating handle, which then rotated the bolt to unlock it by means of a cam and then open it. A return spring drove it back, collecting a cartridge from the box magazine and then locking the bolt once more. Chambered for the 7-mm Spanish Mauser cartridge, used by many Central and South American armies at that time, the Mondragon was beautifully made and worked well, and it was introduced into the Mexican Army in 1908. SIG then went on to make more for sale to any interested armies, and even developed a model with a larger magazine and a bipod as a light machine gun, but there were few takers – it was probably expensive, and there were many armies who were against the whole idea of automatic rifles, fearing that the soldiers would simply blast away all their ammunition in the first few minutes of battle. SIG were eventually to get rid of all their Mondragon rifles in 1915, when the fledgling German air force needed automatic weapons for their early observing aircraft – the Mondragon made a good defensive weapon until a machine gun and mounting had been devized. After that, they were given to snipers on the Western Front, but the mechanism of the Mondragon rifle was never designed with the mud of Flanders in mind, and there they were less successful.

The next practical design came from Russia, and it demonstrated where most of the difficulties of designing automatic rifles lay, though not many people were smart enough to see it. Vladimir Federov was a researcher and designer working for the Russian military authorities, and he made a special study of automatic weapons. By 1905 he had managed to convert the standard Mosin-Nagant bolt-action rifle into a blowback automatic weapon, but he soon dropped the idea because he had a vision – he wanted to make a true automatic rifle, one which would give every soldier a machine gun. Until then, the automatic rifles which had been developed were, strictly speaking, self-loading – they were not, like a machine gun, capable of firing continuously while the trigger was pressed. They fired one shot for each trigger pull and reloaded after each shot (the SIG variation of the Mondragon was a private venture of theirs, the rifle being a self-loader). Federov wanted to produce a weapon which would, if required, act either as a self-loader or as a machine gun. What prevented this was simply the power of the contemporary cartridges.

Most of the armies of the world, by now, used a similar cartridge – one of about 8 mm caliber, and with a hefty propelling charge which allowed them to shoot out to 2,000 yards range and more. Controlling such a rifle was difficult enough with single shots, but automatic fire would be completely uncontrollable unless the weapon was, like a machine gun, firmly mounted on a tripod. And Federov wanted the infantryman to be able to fire from the hip or the shoulder. As a result of the Russo-Japanese War, the Russians also had a large stock of Japanese 6.5-mm rifle cartridges. These were smaller than the usual cartridges used by Western nations, principally because the Japanese soldier was a smaller man and required something with less recoil. They were also a much better shape, being slender, rimless and with slightly necked cases, whereas the 7.62-mm Russian cartridge was a thick, rimmed, abruptly necked design which was extremely awkward to feed from a magazine. So Federov took this 6.5-mm cartridge and developed a rifle around it. It was recoil-operated, had a curved 25-shot magazine, a forward hand grip and fired at 600 rounds per minute in the automatic mode, or single shots as desired. He perfected this design in 1916, production began in 1917, and then the October Revolution stopped it before it had got into its stride. But once the Civil War was more or less over, the factory was reopened in 1919, and some 9,000 were constructed and issued before it was phased out of production in 1924. They were widely used in the aftermath of the Civil War, and Federov continued developing the design for some years, but hardly any of these weapons have ever been seen outside Russia, and very few remain.

The Federov, then, was the first successful automatic rifle, but it was almost unknown outside Russia. Elsewhere, designers were still hard at work trying to develop weapons which would accept the regulation cartridges of the various armies, and not doing very well at it. Some were smart enough to persuade their masters of the problem and get them to accept a smaller cartridge – one such was J. D. Pedersen, a designer working at Springfield Arsenal for the US Army. He managed to persuade Springfield to develop a rimless .276-caliber cartridge and then designed his rifle around that. The rifle used a toggle similar to that of the Luger pistol, but one which did not lock rigidly behind the bolt – instead, the hinges were so placed that the explosion force on the cartridge case would slowly force the toggle open, so that the rifle was actually a delayed blowback weapon. And that led to an interesting problem.

When a weapon is fired the cartridge case is expanded tightly against the inner wall of the chamber by the pressure of the explosion – this is necessary in order to seal the rear end of the weapon against a leakage of the propelling gas. The case is made of brass or steel, and is carefully designed so that the metal will expand under pressure to seal, but will contract once the pressure drops so that the empty case can be extracted. Where the cartridge case is parallel-sided, there are rarely any problems. But a long, thin, tapering, bottlenecked case in a blowback weapon can cause severe problems. The case will expand tightly against the walls, but due to its shape and the restrictive neck and the softness of the case around the neck, the pressure will not drop fast enough to allow the case to shrink back to its original size before the breech-block begins to open and extract the case. So we have the case stuck firmly to the wall at its mouth, and the bolt hooked into the extraction rim and pulling with considerable force on the other end. Either the extractor tears through the rim and leaves the case halfway out of the chamber, or it tears the case in half, ejects the rear half and leaves the front half in the chamber. Either way, you have a seriously jammed gun.

There was nothing new about this problem – it had been encountered before, and the solution was well-known. You lubricate the case – a film of oil will prevent the case adhering too tightly to the wall and will ease the subsequent extraction. By the mid-1920s, when Pedersen was doing his designing, this was well-known, and it was the answer Pedersen chose. He wax-lubricated his cases, and the rifle worked perfectly.

Unfortunately, armies do not like lubricated ammunition, as it tends to gather dust and stick in the chamber if oiled, or the wax peels off in storage and causes problems. So while the US Army were enthusiastic about Pedersen's rifle, they were less happy about the ammunition. Meanwhile, there was another designer hard at work in Springfield Arsenal, also with the .276 cartridge, though he chose to do without the wax because he had developed a design with a locked breech. His name was John C. Garand.

US troops in the South
Pacific in World War II
armed with the M1
Garand, the first general-
issue semi-automatic
rifle in any army.

Garand was an engineer who, during World War I, had designed a machine gun and submitted it to the US War Department. The design appeared promising, and he was invited to continue his development under the supervision of the National Bureau of Standards.

The design came to the notice of Springfield Arsenal, and they were sufficiently impressed to offer him a post as a designer, which he took up in 1919, remaining there until his retirement in 1953. Shortly after he settled in to his new job he began working on an automatic rifle for the .276 cartridge, and when Pedersen's design was turned down because of its need for lubricated cartridges, Garand's design took over as the favorite for possible adoption. He originally perfected a system in which the primer cap sat back in the cartridge due to internal pressure and thus pushed the firing pin back and, by various linkages, unlocked the breech. This worked quite well, but the idea was turned down because it demanded an entirely new type of ammunition – a cartridge with a special primer which could move backwards. He then started again, using conventional ammunition, and his new rifle used a gas piston to drive an operating rod which was linked to the bolt by a cam groove. As the rod moved back under gas pressure, the groove ran across a stud in the bolt, revolving it to unlock and then opening it. A return spring drove it back to collect a cartridge from the magazine and load. As the bolt went back it cocked an internal hammer, which was released by the trigger to hit a firing pin in the bolt and fire the cartridge. The only odd feature was Garand's use of a Mannlicher-type clip holding eight rounds – this was dropped in as a complete unit, a follower arm pushed the rounds up in the clip until the last one had been fired, and then, as the bolt opened after the last shot, the clip was automatically ejected and the bolt remained open ready for a fresh clip to be loaded.

Garand's improved design passed its trials with flying colors, and was formally accepted as the future standard rifle for the US Army in 1932, but no sooner was the decision taken than Gen MacArthur, Chief of Staff, rescinded it. He pointed out that the US Army had several million rounds of .30 ammunition in store, and that there was a considerable manufacturing base laid out for the production of .30 ammunition. Moreover, the army were far from convinced that .276 was an improvement on the .30 cartridge. Would Mr Garand, therefore, be so kind as to re-design his rifle to fire the standard .30 ammunition? I expect Mr Garand was less than pleased, but he set to work, produced a new rifle, had it tested and approved, and in 1936 the Garand rifle was standardized as the Rifle .30 M1, the first semi-automatic rifle to become standard issue in a major army. In fact, due to the shortage of funds which afflicted many armies in 1936, general issue was impossible, and it was not until 1941 that the bolt action Springfield M1903 was completely replaced in frontline units.

The Garand appeared again in the Korean War of 1950-53. Here a sniper, his Garand fitted with a flash hider and telescope sight, is protected by his buddy, seen loading a clip into his standard M1 Garand.

There were, of course, attempts by other forces to produce an automatic rifle as their standard weapon, but few got beyond the prototype stage. One which did succeed in bringing two rifles into limited service was the Soviet Army. The Federov had, by this time, been more or less forgotten, and the bolt-action Mosin-Nagant of 1895 – periodically revamped – was the standard arm. The Soviets felt that it was time this was replaced, and that replacement by an automatic would put the Red Army well ahead of its potential opponents, so the request was put out to their several design bureaux. Most of these had been working steadily away at automatic rifle designs since 1920, and thus there were a number of ideas put forward – the best of these appeared to be a design by Sergey Simonov, and in 1936 it was selected to be the standard Soviet rifle.

The AVS-36 (*Avtomaticheskaya Vintovka Simonova*) was gas-operated, using a piston mounted above the barrel to unlock and open the bolt – the locking system was rather unusual, relying upon a vertically-moving block to lock the bolt, and its carrier securely to the receiver of the rifle. It was produced as a selective-fire weapon, one capable of delivering either single shots or automatic fire. By the end of 1938 some 35,000 had been produced, but by that time complaints had started to come in. The muzzle blast was excessive, probably because a muzzle brake had been fitted to try and reduce the recoil, and there were also troubles with feeding from the magazine, though this was principally the fault of the elderly rimmed cartridge case, never designed for use in automatic weapons. Indeed, most of the complaints had been evident in the trials, but rather than wait, it was decided to go on with the Simonov and, at the same time, look for a better design.

The better design appeared in 1938 with the Tokarev SVT-38. This was also gas-operated, a short-stroke gas piston giving the bolt carrier an impulsive blow and the momentum of the bolt and carrier then taking them back to perform the reloading cycle. Two lugs on the bolt rode in grooves in the bolt carrier – as the bolt closed up against the chamber and stopped, the carrier continued forward and the grooves forced the lugs to drive the rear end of the bolt down to wedge in front of a hardened steel bar in the floor of the receiver, so locking the bolt securely. It was chambered for the same rimmed 7.62-mm cartridge as the SVS-36 and fed from a shorter 10-shot box magazine which appears to have given less trouble than the curved 15-shot box of the SVS-36.

The Tokarev design was formally adopted in February 1939, but by that time Simonov had appeared with a redesign which, he claimed, did away with the problems of the 1936 rifle. Some discussion ensued, and finally Stalin himself weighed in – all work on other designs was to stop and the Tokarev was to go into mass-production forthwith. Four-and-a-half million rifles had to be delivered by 1942, or else.

Possibly 150,000 rifles had been made and distributed when Russia went to war with Finland in late 1939, whereupon, like most rifles, they exhibited a crop of defects which had never showed up in testing, though to be fair to Tokarev, it seems that most of them were manufacturing faults, rather than design defects. Production was stopped, modifications incorporated, and production of the SVT-40 improved version began in mid-1940. A million or so had been made by the time of the German invasion in June 1941, and production continued for some time, but eventually it was decided that the Tokarev was too complicated a production task for the situation in which Russia found herself. Cheap and simple sub-machine guns were needed, so the Tokarev production was ended some time in 1943. A number of the rifles were fitted with telescope sights and issued to snipers, since snipers can generally give better care to rifles than the average soldier, and an automatic weapon is an advantage for sniping in that the sniper doesn't have to move his arm to reload, and thus attract attention.

One might have expected that the German Army would also be lusting after a new automatic rifle, but in fact they showed no interest in any immediate solution – they had their eyes on the longer term.

In the 1920s and early 1930s a number of designers had produced weapons using smaller (than usual) cartridges – not smaller in caliber, but smaller in length. Their argument was that by making a shorter cartridge you got a shorter rifle, which was more convenient for the soldier, and you also got a lighter cartridge which meant that the soldier carried less weight or, more likely, carried the same weight, but got more cartridges into it. On the whole, however, soldiers saw immediately that shorter cartridges meant lower power, and that, so far as they were concerned, was the end of the discussion.

When Germany began re-arming, a group of German infantry officers were charged with the task of examining the current small arms field and making recommendations about future weapons. They began by examining the records of combat during World War I, and they soon discovered that while the infantryman was provided with a powerful rifle capable of shooting to 2,000 yards or more, he rarely shot at an enemy at a range greater than 500 yards and, indeed, had great difficulty in even seeing a target at that range. There seemed to be no good reason for burdening the man with a heavy rifle and powerful ammunition when he never used it, and therefore some development work began on a shorter cartridge which would permit the design of a lighter rifle. Moreover, a shorter cartridge, as Federov had shown with his Automat, allowed the rifle to be given the power of automatic fire which was controllable, thus immeasurably increasing the firepower of the infantry squad.

A short cartridge of 7 mm caliber was designed and tested, but before work could begin on a suitable rifle, the design team ran into the same trouble that had stopped Garand in his tracks – the authorities pointed out that they had several million rounds of standard 7.92-mm Mauser cartridges in store, and a sizeable industry geared up to produce them. Moreover, things, by this time, were beginning to look somewhat unstable in Europe, and

A sequence from a 1914 newspaper, showing how to load the Mauser Gewehr 98 rifle; Top left – take a charger of five cartridges; bottom left – insert it into the charger guides; top right – press down the cartridges with the thumb, into the magazine; bottom right – close the bolt.

changing calibers in the face of a forthcoming war was not considered wise. The cartridge designers, certain their reasoning was right and that their day would come, re-designed the cartridge in 7.92 mm caliber so that it could be manufactured on the existing machinery with slight modification – they then let it be known around the various gun design houses that a short 7.92-mm cartridge was available for experimenting and went on to other things.

And in 1939 the war began and there was no shortage of other things for them to do. Then, in 1940, came an urgent demand from the German Army for a semi-automatic rifle, and since speed was of the essence, nobody thought of anything but using the standard 7.92-mm Mauser cartridge. Two designs appeared, one from Mauser and the other from the Carl Walther Waffenfabrik, who had hitherto been known principally for their pistols, but it was the Mauser which was turned down and the Walther was chosen for development as the Gewehr 41(W). It was gas-operated in a rather unusual manner which harked back to Browning's early experiments – the muzzle was surrounded by a cup which deflected the blast back and onto the face of a piston which surrounded the barrel. This was driven back to unlock and open the bolt, and being returned by a spring, it reloaded the chamber. It worked, but it was cumbersome, badly balanced and muzzle heavy, slow to reload the magazine, and expensive and slow to manufacture. It was adopted in early 1942, some 8,000 were made and mostly used on the Eastern Front, but it was not popular, and the army looked for a replacement.

While this had been going on the Luftwaffe (the German air force) had asked for a selective-fire rifle for their paratroopers, demanding a length under one metre and a weight less than that of the standard Mauser 98 rifle, with the ability to fire the 7.92-mm Mauser cartridge at full-automatic. The

Army told them not to be ridiculous, such a combination being impossible. But the Luftwaffe was run by Field-Marshal Hermann Goering, a powerful man who usually got what he wanted, and if his boys wanted a rifle then they would have one, no matter what the Army had to say about it. The specification went out to various companies, and the *Rheinmetall-Borsig AG*, who normally built artillery, took up the challenge – and succeeded.

In spite of all the experts, Louis Stange, their designer, produced a rifle 937 mm long, weighing 4.3 kg (400 gm more than the Mauser 98k rifle) and capable of firing at 800 rounds per minute. It was an odd-looking weapon, being all-metal in its construction, laid out in a straight line with the butt at the end of the receiver, a box magazine fitting into the left side, a steeply raked pistol-grip and a spike bayonet. It went into production in 1942, being made by the Haenel company, since *Rheinmetall* had no production facilities, and it has been estimated that about 2,000 were made. The paratroops were happy with it, but by this time there was rather less urgency than in 1940 as they had been badly mauled during the invasion of Crete in 1941, suffering such a high percentage of casualties that Hitler forbade airborne operations thereafter – the paratroopers spent the rest of the war as ordinary infantry. And with the loss of their special role, and with the gradual decline in importance of Goering, they found it less easy to make demands and get them filled. Nevertheless, the *Fallschirmgewehr* 42 – their own special rifle – managed to survive. The first design had to be modified – to obtain the desired lightness it used high-grade manganese steel, and this was scarce. There were one or two other complaints as a result of combat use, so a complete re-design was done. The new weapon was longer and heavier, had a bipod beneath the muzzle, a cover over the ejection port which kept out the dirt, and a wooden butt and fore-end. The stroke of the gas piston and bolt were

A sort of a sub-machine gun produced by Mauser in the 1930s; this is the standard military pistol modified to take a removable 20-shot magazine and with a selector switch on the side to permit automatic fire. Fitted with its usual holster-stock, it was a poor substitute for a Bergmann or MP38.

made longer to soak up some of the recoil force, which slowed the rate of fire to about 750 rounds a minute, and caused less breakage of internal parts. Production of this weapon began in late 1943, and about 6,000 were made before materials shortages, and the declining importance of the airborne forces in Germany, brought manufacture to a halt. But it was an important milestone in firearms development, even if only for showing what the limits were when using full-power cartridges.

The German Army, probably muttering the German equivalent of "I told you so", turned their back on the development of the FG42 and applied once more to the gun companies for a lightweight automatic rifle, and this time either the army or the gunmakers recalled the 7-mm short cartridge which had been put together before the war. Both Walther and Haenel produced prototypes, trials showing that both were effective, and about 1,000 of each were made for troop trials. These showed that the Haenel was easier to make, simpler to maintain and more resistant to operation in adverse conditions, so the Walther design was dropped and Haenel went into production with the *Maschinen Pistole* 43. According to legend – and probably true – Hitler was opposed to the short cartridge concept, and forbade the development of a new rifle, so the army put it into production as a "Machine Pistol", thus ensuring that the monthly production figures appeared under sub-machine guns, and as Hitler approved of sub-machine guns, he was happy. By the time he discovered this, the new weapon was such a success that he put a brave face on it and christened the new weapon the *Sturmgewehr*, or assault rifle, a name which has stuck to this class of weapon ever since.

On the other side of the Atlantic the Americans were faced with a different problem. They were, in 1940, planning for a large army if, as seemed likely, they got involved in the war. Large armies need a lot of weapons, but not all the soldiers need the same weapon. There was very little point in giving a truck driver, who might never be called upon to fight except in a gross emergency, a powerful infantry rifle such as the Garand. You could give him a pistol, but you need a good deal of training and practice to be of much use with a pistol at any range greater than arm's length. Mortar men, artillerymen and others needed a defensive arm, but again the full-sized rifle was too cumbersome and tended to get left in the truck, and thus wasn't handy when needed. Pistols, again, were no use – these men want to keep an enemy well away while they make good their departures. What was needed, decided the army, was a light rifle – something light enough to be carried rather than left in the truck, but not large enough to get in the way of a man operating a mortar. Light enough to be easy to aim and fire, heavy enough to deliver a decent bullet. By late September 1940 the decision had been taken, and it was decreed that the weapon would fire a cartridge "similar to that of the Winchester self-loading .32 cartridge" – in other words a straight-sided rimless case carrying a bullet of about 110 grains weight, with a muzzle velocity of 2,000 ft per second. The Winchester company was given the job of developing the cartridge, and the design of the rifle was thrown open to a number of companies – Springfield Armory, Reising, Winchester, Harrington and Richardson, Savage, Auto-Ordnance and others less well-known.

Winchester had an edge as, earlier in 1940, they had developed an automatic rifle and offered it to the US Marines and the British. Both declined, the Marines because the Garand was, they thought, coming next week, and the British because the Germans, they thought, were coming the next day, and they were not about to get involved with an entirely new weapon under those circumstances. This rifle used a short-stroke gas piston system which had been invented some years before by a man named David Williams. In this system, instead of having a long gas cylinder under the barrel, with a piston traveling back and forth for as much distance as it took to open the bolt and eject the spent case, there was a very short cylinder – indeed, little more than a block of steel – under the barrel, which housed a captive piston about half an inch long. The gas, entering this "cylinder" at high velocity, gave the piston head a powerful thrust backwards. The tail end of this piston, outside the steel block, touched the front end of an operating rod, and when the piston was impeled by the gas, it gave the operating rod an impulsive blow which was sufficient to drive it all the length needed. The operating rod ended in a cam, very much the same as the Garand rifle, and this acted on a lug on the bolt to revolve, and then withdraw the bolt. A spring was loaded, a hammer cocked, and then the spring thrust the operating rod back to close the bolt, loading a new cartridge on the way.

In the summer of 1940 things were not too desperate in the USA, which allowed sufficient spare time for a couple of Winchester employees to take the mechanism of this rifle and see if they could build a nice light hunting rifle around it. They pottered along on this project when there was nothing better to do, with the blessing of the company. Now, when the demand for the new army rifle arose, Edwin Pugsley, the factory superintendent, remembered these two men and their light rifle, called them in, gave them the new cartridge, and suggested that they drop everything else and complete their design as a light military weapon. Since this involved very little more than redimensioning various parts to fit the cartridge, it was not long before they had a working prototype, and when the army called for the competing designs to be tested on 15 September, Winchester was able to produce a finished article, whereas the other contenders were still in the advanced prototype stage. Winchester therefore received the contract, and the M1 Carbine was born. As for the oft-repeated legend of "Carbine Williams", apart from the fact that his gas piston, invented some years before, was used, he had nothing whatsoever to do with the carbine design.

The M1 Carbine, one of the World War II success stories and a highly popular weapon even today, used by many police forces around the world.

The army had originally asked for the Carbine to be a selective-fire weapon, but some preliminary tests in May 1941 decided them against the idea, and the M1 was strictly a self-loading gun, using a 15-shot magazine. For the purpose for which it was designed – self-defense by non-frontline troops – it was excellent. But its primary characteristic – light weight – made it attractive to the GI, and many went to great lengths to get rid of their Garands and obtain a carbine, whereupon it became apparent that it was far from being an ideal frontline weapon, since it simply did not have enough power to stop a determined attacker, and the troops demanded the ability to fire automatically, assuming that if one bullet wouldn't stop him, half a dozen might. The army eventually bowed to the uproar, and the M2 carbine, with a selector switch allowing automatic fire and a 30-round magazine, appeared late in 1944.

There was, of course, another alternative to the rifle, or pistol, for those people who only needed a self-defense weapon – the sub-machine gun. And since its birth in World War I, the sub-machine gun had suffered a tedious and painful adolescence. The association of the Thompson gun with the Irish Republican Army and the underworld of Chicago did nothing for its image, even though it was adopted in small numbers by the US Marines, and the sub-machine gun was looked on by most soldiers as a "gangster weapon". They simply could not see any tactical application for such a gun. Admittedly, the weapon had been born as a military weapon, for use in a particular tactical situation – the breaching of a loosely-held, but powerful, defensive line – but this was a situation which, it was generally held, had been unique and would be unlikely to appear again. And if it didn't appear again, what was the point of the sub-machine gun? Every other tactical scenario they could visualize was amply provided for by rifles, light machine guns and pistols. Even the US Marines originally bought it as a compact weapon for guarding mail trains, which was hardly a military tactical function.

Nevertheless, one or two designers persisted with the idea, assuming that sooner or later its virtues would become apparent. Beretta of Italy had converted all the original Vilar-Perosa weapons into stocked sub-machine guns, and these were issued to the Italian Army, but since they looked like rifles – they even had bayonets – unless the magazine was fitted, most people never realized they existed. Hugo Schmeisser in Germany had made some slight improvements to the Bergmann MP18, but it was hardly a best-seller. In Finland an unknown designer called Aimo Lahti saw a place for the sub-machine gun in the Arctic forests of Finland and developed an excellent model which the Finnish Army adopted, but again it saw very little acceptance beyond that. And, contrary to common belief, very few sub-machine guns were ever used in the Spanish Civil War – I have searched through volumes of reminiscences without finding a single one mentioned, and recent researches carried out into the supply of weapons to the Republicans during the war indicate that no sub-machine guns at all were bought.

Even the German Army, popularly believed to be in the forefront of weapons development, was dubious about the beast. In the early 1920s an engineering company was set up in Erfurt, Germany – the *Erfurter Maschinenwerk B.Giepel Gmbh*, shortened to Erma. The proprietor, Berthold Giepel, employed a brilliant designer, Heinrich Vollmer, and between them they developed a self-contained bolt unit in which the bolt, firing pin and return spring were all enclosed in a telescoping tube, so that when the gun was opened for dismantling, only one piece had to be lifted

INNOVATIONS

Two GIs in Normandy, 1944, demonstrating how not to go to war; the Carbine and the Colt pistol were never intended as hunting or assault weapons, purely as self-defense weapons, and to use them like this on a patrol would be foolhardy. But they were light and handy, and that probably counted more than theoretical considerations.

out instead of the individual bits cascading out all over the floor. They incorporated this into a simple sub-machine gun with a wooden stock and side-mounted magazine, similar to the Bergmann in many respects, but with a unique vertical forward hand grip carved in one piece with the stock. This sold moderately well to police forces and then in 1935 a long-barreled version with a bayonet was adopted by the Yugoslavian Army, and Erma received a useful contract. But try as he might, Giepel could get no change out of the German Army. They could see no tactical use for it.

Not daunted, and supported by the Yugoslavian contract, Giepel and Vollmer sat down again and planned their next design – they wanted to get away from the now-traditional wooden stock, perforated jacket, side magazine format and try something new. And then, in 1936, there came a call from the army – they were setting up something new in the form of an armored division, which involved soldiers inside tanks and troop-carriers where conventional rifles were inconvenient. Could they perhaps have another look at the Erma sub-machine gun? "Better than that", said Giepel, "have a look at our new design; all-metal, folding stock, short barrel, magazine underneath where it acts. as a hand grip, all good 20th-century stuff. Nobody ever made a gun with no wood in before did they? Nobody ever thought of a folding butt before did they? Try it."

The army tried it, and came back and asked for one modification – a bar beneath the barrel with a step in it, so that when the barrel was thrust through the firing-port of a troop carrying vehicle and fired, the step would lock on the outside of the port and the recoil would not drive the barrel back inside the vehicle while the gun was still firing – one is inclined to wonder what sort of a disastrous accident took place to give rise to that idea! And once that was done, the design was approved as the *Maschinen Pistole* 38 (MP38), and went into production in early 1938.

The MP38 ushered in a completely new era of gunmaking. Gone was the polished walnut, the shining brass, the chunks of intricately-shaped solid steel. The receiver of the MP38 was a commercial drawn steel tube, machined away for lightness and slotted here and there; the shoulder stock was a pressed-steel tubular structure with a steel end, hinged so that it folded under the body of the gun and still allowed it to fire; the hand grip and trigger unit were an aluminium casting requiring the minimum of finishing. And yet, for all that, it had an elegant and purposeful look which made it one of the most photogenic weapons – no film or TV play about Germany in World War II would be considered authentic unless somebody appears carrying an MP38.

Or an MP40 – most people can't distinguish between them. War service in the Polish campaign showed that the MP38 had one defect – a defect which affected all sub-machine guns, more or less. If the loaded magazine was in place and the weapon was dropped on its butt, such as a soldier might do if he was jumping out of a truck and used the gun to support him on landing, then the shock could cause the bolt to fly down in the receiver, not far enough to be held by the sear, after which it would fly back, collect a round from the magazine and fire it – to the detriment of the man holding it or, more usually, to some other innocent standing yards away. This was simply cured by making the cocking handle a long pin and drilling a hole in the opposite side of the receiver – when the bolt was closed on an empty chamber, driving the cocking handle inward sent its other end into the hole, so locking the bolt very securely forward. An MP38 modified in this way became an MP38/40.

The other fault with the MP38 was that it took too long to make, and the Polish campaign suggested that the rate of attrition of weapons in modern warfare might be somewhat high. So Erma did a redesign, not changing the method of operation or the general appearance, but changing the materials and method of construction. Instead of machined steel, there came stamped steel welded together – instead of cast aluminium, sheet-steel brazed and spot-welded, and the whole weapon was now designed with ease of manufacture uppermost. Strangely, this simplification actually put up the price – an official list of costs on 1 February 1943 has the MP38 at 57 Reichsmarks (about $19.75 at 1939 rates) and the MP40 at 60RM ($20.75). One dollar may not sound much, but multiply by the million-and-a-half or so MP40 made, and it soon adds up.

The strange thing about the MP38/40 tribe is that whenever they appear on the movies or TV somebody always says "Look, a Schmeisser. . ." And why this should be is something of a mystery. As we have seen it was designed by Vollmer and Giepel, and made by Ermawerk. No member of the Schmeisser family had anything whatsoever to do with it. Later in the war, when production was needed, the Haenel company were sub-contracted to manufacture the MP40, and it so happened that the factory superintendent was Hugo Schmeisser. But by that time it was already known to the Allies as "the Schmeisser", and nobody knew of Hugo's peripheral attachment to the weapon until the war was over. It is one of the greatest puzzles in the firearms world.

Oh yes – how do you tell an MP38 from an MP40? It's all in the corrugations. The MP38 receiver is corrugated along its length in order to lighten it, but the magazine housing is smooth, with a large hole in it. The MP40 receiver is smooth, but the magazine housing is corrugated and has no hole in it. There are other, smaller, differences, and of course they have MP38 or MP40 stamped into them, but the corrugations, or lack of them, identifies them at a distance.

As the war clouds gathered, so a lot of armies began taking a second look at the sub-machine gun, particularly armies which needed weapons to equip a hurriedly conscripted force. Sub-machine guns, even the "traditional" types made of expensively-machined steel and carefully carved wood, were cheaper and quicker to make than rifles, and they were usually simpler to operate. But it all came back to the question "How do you

The Erma MP38, first modern sub-machine gun; first weapon to dispense with wooden fittings, first weapon to have a folding butt.

intend to use them?" The Russians had no doubts – a cheap and cheerful sub-machine gun was all you could expect a conscripted peasant to master, and the only tactics they would ever learn would be to get out of the trench and go after the enemy, so a close-quarter weapon was fine by them. The British had a different view, and eventually reached the conclusion that it would be a good weapon for infantry fighting patrols, who usually performed all their fighting at close quarters and in a hell of a rush. The French were of a similar opinion, feeling that such patrols would be useful for filling in the gaps between the Maginot Line forts.

In 1939 the market in sub-machine guns was far from crowded. There were a number of designs being touted around, but that was all they were – designs. Actual hardware was scarce, and the British Ordnance Board summed it up in late 1939 by saying "We are down to two reliable weapons – the Finnish Suomi and the American Thompson. The Finns will not part with their Suomis, and the Thompson is grossly expensive". So they had to buy the Thompson. What made the Thompson expensive was simply the fact that everybody was after them, and the highest bidder was going to get them – and that was France. And what everybody was bidding for were guns assembled from what was left of the 15,000 sets of parts which Colt had made for Auto-Ordnance in 1921! Seeing the demand, Auto-Ordnance set up a factory and began making Thompsons as fast as they could go, and subcontracted the Savage Arms company to make them as well.

The fall of France in 1940 laid Britain open to invasion by Germany, whose army sat less than 30 miles away across the English Channel. Submachine guns were needed for airfield guards, Home Guards and, generally, as a means of getting firepower into as many hands as possible in a

short time. The Thompsons ordered by France and undelivered were diverted to Britain, but that was far from enough, so plans were laid to manufacture a weapon in Britain. The easiest way, it was thought, would be simply to copy an existing design, and the one selected to be copied, because it seemed to be the simplest, was the Bergmann MP28, an improved version of the World War I weapon. But, as is always the case when any nation sets out to copy another's design, it had to be "improved" first. The resulting gun was known as the Lanchester, in honour of the man who did the re-design, and it must be said that the changes were relatively small and largely consisted of manufacturing short-cuts. But it still took time to get into production, and time, in 1940, was something the British didn't have a great deal of.

While the Lanchester was in the planning stage two designers as the Royal Small Arms Factory at Enfield set about designing something which would be easy to make, reliable and effective. They produced the N.O.T. 40/1 in January 1941, and before the month was out it had been thoroughly tested and approved for mass-production. The title was cumbersome and some shorter name was needed, so they took the initials of the two designers, Maj R. V. Shepherd and Mr H. J. Turpin, and the first two letters of the place of origin, and came up with the Sten gun. By July 1941 it was in full production – the Lanchester production had also begun, but the Sten was so much easier and cheaper to make that the Lanchester was issued only to the Royal Navy, and once their relatively small requirements had been met, production was stopped.

The Sten gun, the "Stench gun", the "Woolworth gun", the "Plumber's Friend" – it had a lot of names, none of them complimentary, but for all that men swore at it, they also swore by it, for it had one great virtue – it was so simple that practically nothing could go wrong with it. Bake it, freeze it, drench it in mud or blast it with sand, a quick wipe of the hand and the Sten would fire. The only defect was in the magazine – officially it held 32 rounds, but wise men only ever put 30 in it as those last two could overload the spring, and cause a feed jam.

The Mark 1 model still had some pretense of elegance – a wooden butt, a wooden fore-grip, a simple flash hider/compensator on the muzzle. But it was soon recognized that these were trimmings, and the Mark 2, which was the definitive model, did away with everything which wasn't vital. The basic component, upon which everything else was built, was the tubular receiver. Into the front went the barrel, held there by a retaining sleeve screwed in by hand and which, being perforated, also acted as the front grip. Into the back of the tube went the bolt, with a fixed firing pin, followed by a return spring, both held in place by a bayonet cap on the back end of the tube. Beneath the tube was a sheet-metal box with the trigger mechanism, a simple linkage with a crossbolt selector which gave automatic fire when pushed one way and single shots when pushed the other. At the front of the tube were two slots, one on each side, and a magazine housing fitted on a sleeve with a spring catch. When turned to the vertical, the sleeve closed both slots. When turned up to the left and locked, the magazine could be inserted so that it fed through the left slot, and the spent cases were ejected through the right slot. There was a butt, a single metal tube with a flat shoulder-piece at the end, which was attached to the back end of the tube by the bayonet cap and a spring. There was a triangular piece of metal at the front end acting as a front sight, and another piece of metal with a hole in it at the back end acting as a backsight. That was the lot.

But it wasn't quite as simple as it looked – the Sten worked on a rather ingenious system called "advanced primer ignition" which went a long way to saving weight and making automatic fire controllable. To fire, you pulled back the bolt until it was held by the trigger sear. When the trigger was pressed the bolt flew forward and collected a cartridge from the magazine, shoving it into the chamber. The bolt face and the feedway were carefully designed so that the cartridge gradually lined up with the axis of the bolt as it was fed forward, but the cap never actually got in front of the firing pin until the cartridge had entered the chamber. Once the cartridge did get into the chamber, it slowed up because the chamber dimensions made it a relatively tight fit. The bolt hadn't slowed up though, and as it thrust forward so the firing pin hit the cap and the cartridge fired – while the bolt was still moving forward. So the pressure in the chamber, thrusting back on the cartridge case as well as pushing forward the bullet, had first of all to stop the forward movement of the bolt, then start it moving backwards.

Now, if the gun had been designed to fire when the bolt was stationary, then the bolt would have to be heavy enough to resist the impulse of the

cartridge explosion for long enough to allow the bullet to leave the muzzle. But by making it fire while the bolt was still moving it became possible to make the bolt about 25 percent lighter, due to the extra work being done by the explosion – not just overcoming the inertia of a stationary mass, but first arresting a moving mass, then reversing it. In addition to absorbing more energy, this also absorbed time, giving the bullet ample time to get clear before the arrest and reversal had taken place. Moreover, the energy so absorbed allowed the bolt to have a shorter travel against the return spring, so that the whole gun could be shorter. All of which added up to a shorter, lighter gun with the same power.

Britain devoted an entire ordnance factory to the Sten gun, turning out 20,000 guns a week until the war ended – mass-production got the price down to about $10 each, and millions were distributed throughout the various Resistance Organisations set up on the Continent to harry the occupying Germans. From there they spread all over, and it will be a long time before the last Sten gun goes to the scrap yard. Not that they were meant to last this long – indeed, the Sten was probably the first gun to break the "gunsmith's barrier" to produce a gun which, with no thought for appearance, proportion, grace, or high-class finish, was simply a device for killing people. Once it wore out, it could be thrown away – it was cheaper to make a new one than to try and repair the broken one.

The Russians appreciated this argument as well, and their sub-machine guns were almost as basic as the Sten, even though their design and development took years rather than weeks. Soviet development of a sub-machine gun began in 1927 with F. V. Tokarev developing a gun which fired the Nagant revolver cartridge. This seemed to work quite well, and in 1928 instructions were given to make ten of varying barrel lengths and other details, for tests. But the Artillery Commission now ruled that any sub-machine gun had to fire the same 7.62-mm cartridge as the forthcoming automatic pistol, so it was back to the drawing board for all concerned.

The Degtyarev-designed PPD-40 sub-machine gun which armed a large part of the Soviet Army in 1942.

In 1930 three designs firing the 7.62-mm rimless cartridge were tried out – all were overweight, all fired far too fast and all tended to open the breech before the pressure had dropped. "Off you go and try again", said the Commission. Eventually, in 1934 a Degtyarev design was approved, but few were made and fewer issued – by 1939 the few thousand sub-machine guns in the Soviet army had all been withdrawn and were in store, since nobody could make up his mind who was to use them, or how. Nevertheless, during these years the Degtyarev (which, to be honest, had been issued far too soon, before all the bugs had been found) was worked over and improved, so that by the time things began to look dangerous, it was in a fit condition to be issued as the PPD-40.

Degtyarev's 1934 design used a 25-round box magazine and, one supposes from looking at it, leaned heavily on the Bergmann for its inspiration. But 25 rounds was not considered sufficient, and he developed an ingenious 70-round drum magazine which had a peculiar vertical extension so that it could fit into the magazine housing designed for the box magazine. During the 1939/40 Winter War the Soviets found themselves confronted by Finns armed with the Suomi – a far better weapon in the frozen forests than the Soviet rifle. The 1934 guns were brought out from store, and once the campaign was over, Degtyarev made some final changes to produce the PPD-40 – this used a drum magazine without the extension, which was more or less a copy of the Suomi magazine, and did away with the box magazine entirely. It went into production again, but it was soon realized that if war was coming, then the PPD-40 was not the right weapon – it was too slow to make, not having been designed for mass-production techniques.

One feature of Soviet weapons design is that there were always a number of different teams attacking any particular problem, and when one team's solution was chosen, the others didn't simply give up and look for something else to do – they carried on developing their own idea, intent upon out-performing the chosen model. This was probably due to the fact that throughout the Communist period almost every design accepted for service was found wanting after it had gone into production, by which time a competing design had been perfected and took over from it. So the teams had a pretty good idea that whoever was first selected would probably be de-selected fairly soon, and they would be in with a chance.

Whatever the politics behind it, multiple design teams were the system, and now, with long faces being pulled at the PPD-40 production figures, along came G. S. Shpagin with his idea for a sub-machine gun. Mechanically it differed little from Degtyarev's design, being a simple blowback bolt and return spring system – its major difference lay in its design and method of manufacture. Shpagin had seen the need for mass-production in wartime, and he designed his gun to be built from steel stampings, welded and brazed together.

The only complicated part was the barrel – although chromium-plated internally to reduce the rate of wear, even this could be turned out on standard barrel-making machines used for the army's rifle, and it was dimensioned so that one rifle-barrel length could be cut in half to make two sub-machine gun barrels. The perforated barrel jacket extended forward of the muzzle and became a compensator, and the gun was designed to use the same 71-round magazine which was already in production for the PPD-40. The gun passed its tests successfully, and on 21 December 1940 it was officially adopted as the PPSh-41, although production did not begin until the late summer of 1941. How many million were eventually made has never been disclosed, but certainly the PPSh-41 became the trade-mark of the Soviet soldier in the same manner that the MP38 became that of the German.

The design teams, though, still kept working, and now came the third Soviet sub-machine gun design – that of A. I. Sudayev – which had a peculiar history. Sudayev was a young designer who had gone into the weapons field after his military service, and was working in Leningrad when the city was besieged by the Germans. There, he perfected his sub-machine gun design in a rather unusual manner – instead of being guided by tactical requirements, he was constrained by what materials and what manufacturing facilities were available within Leningrad. As a result, he produced one of the simplest designs ever seen – a simple blowback weapon constructed of sheet-metal stampings, riveted and welded together. The only wood used was on the hand grip, and the only other non-metallic material in the design was a piece of leather acting as the buffer to stop the bolt's rearward movement. It used a 35-round curved magazine which had recently been developed for the PPSh-41 and, of course, fired the standard 7.62-mm pistol cartridge. The body of the gun extended forward to form a perforated

The Story
of the Gun

barrel jacket, and a loop of metal in front of the muzzle acted as a muzzle brake. A folding shoulder-stock of metal strips was provided, folding over the top of the weapon.

Sudayev's design went into immediate production and straight out the factory door to the defenders of the city, being virtually tested in combat. It was officially approved as the PPS-42 and Sudayev set about making a few improvements as a result of comments from the frontline. He improved the cartridge ejection system, the folding stock and the safety catch, put in a stronger return spring, made the hand grips of hard rubber and replaced the leather buffer with a fibre pattern. The angle of the magazine housing was changed to improve reliability of the feed, and the resulting weapon became the PPS-43. It went into production in the middle of 1943, and remained in production until 1946. After the siege of Leningrad had been lifted, the PPS-43 had a wider distribution, but in the late 1940s all seem to have been withdrawn, and they were never seen again in Soviet service, although they turned up in large numbers in the hands of foreign forces of Communist persuasion – they were commonly seen in the hands of Chinese and North Korean troops during the Korean War.

Soviet PPSh-41 sub-machine guns discovered in an arms cache in Cambodia in 1970, many years after the Soviet Army had got rid of them.

The third, and some say the best, of the Soviet wartime sub-machine guns was this PPS-42 model, designed and built under siege conditions in Leningrad.

So far as we know, the reason for this sudden abandonment of a very good design was entirely political. The Lenigraders were, quite rightly, proud of their performance in keeping the German Army at bay for something like three years, losing over a million of their population from starvation, illness and combat in the process. And in the postwar years Stalin feared that they were getting a little above themselves. So the whole story of the siege was downgraded, the weapons were removed from sight, and several of the more prominent figures in the siege also vanished. Sudayev died in 1946, only 38 years of age, which was remarkably young for a Soviet designer, most of whom manage to reach their 70s with little trouble.

Early in 1941 the US Army decided that a sub-machine gun was necessary for the infantry and cavalry, and so far as they could see, the only available design was the Thompson. There were a number of other designs on offer, but none had got beyond the prototype phase, and none appeared to promise what they were after – a cheap and effective weapon. An early model of the British Sten gun was obtained and studied, and the logic behind it was appreciated – so much so that Col Rene Studler, chief of the Small Arms Development Branch of the Ordnance Department, called in George Hyde, an engineer who had developed one or two sub-machine gun designs, and Frederick Sampson, chief engineer of the Inland Division of General Motors. Hyde and Sampson then sat down together, Hyde to design a gun and Sampson to modify the design and steer Hyde so that the finished article could be efficiently mass-produced on machinery originally developed for stamping out automobile parts.

The design was ingenious – a simple blowback weapon, with a tubular receiver and an exposed, thin barrel, its appearance led to its nickname of the "Grease Gun". But while designed around the standard American .45 Colt automatic pistol cartridge, it could be easily adapted by changing the

The M3 sub-machine gun, or "Grease Gun", showing its unusual cocking crank handle.

barrel and bolt and fitting an adapter to the magazine housing to fire the 9-mm Parabellum cartridge common in Europe. In this mode, the Sten magazine was to be used, saving the trouble of manufacturing a 9-mm magazine. The whole weapon, apart from the barrel and bolt, was stamped, pressed and welded from sheet steel. It was approved for issue in December 1942 and went into mass-production.

The only unusual feature of the M3, as the new gun was properly known, was the method of cocking. Instead of the usual slot in the side of the receiver with a cocking handle sticking out, the M3 had a crank handle on the right side of the receiver. There was also a hinged cover which snapped over the ejection port – inside this was a projection which either locked the bolt, if it was forward, or prevented a cocked bolt moving forward and firing. To cock the weapon the cover was flipped open and the crank handle pulled back and released. All this was done so that with the ejection port cover closed, there was no aperture through which dirt or dust could enter the inside of the weapon. But experience in the field soon showed that the cocking action wasn't working properly, and it was discovered that the steel used for the cocking device was improperly hardened and soon wore away. A redesign was urgently called for, and the simplest method was to do away with the crank system, make the ejection port cover rather longer, and make a large recessed hole in the bolt. To cock, you simply flipped open the cover, stuck your finger in the hole, and pulled the bolt back. At the same time, some smaller modifications were made, strengthening parts which had been found weak under the stress of combat, and the result was the M3A1 sub-machine gun, approved in December 1944.

While waiting for the M3 to enter production, the Thompson had been purchased in some numbers – they were being made by Auto-Ordnance and also by the Savage Arms company. The engineers at Savage looked long and hard at the Thompson design, particularly the Blish H-Piece and its complexities, and came to the conclusion that the gun would probably work just as well without all that careful machining. So they built a Thompson with a solid breech-block and demonstrated that it worked perfectly well as a simple blowback gun. Note that they did not, as is often said, "take out the H-piece and fire it", because without the H-piece you can't even cock a Thompson, let alone fire it. Auto-Ordnance didn't want to know – the Thompson was their baby and nobody was going to fool around with it, but when Savage told the Army about their modifications, the latter realized that the simpler version would be cheaper and quicker to make, easier to maintain and generally offer an improvement. So the modified design became the Thompson M1, and further modification also simplified the magazine housing and made the gun workable only with the 20-round box magazine – the drum magazine was no longer considered practical. The difference in appearance is simple. The M1928 series original guns have the cocking handle on top of the receiver, while the M1 (and the slightly modified M1A1) have it on the right side.

1963 Montagnard Commandos get ready for a patrol into Vietcong territory, armed with the M3A1 sub-machine gun.

The sub-machine gun had originated in World War I, but only came into prominence during the later global conflict. In a similar fashion, the light machine gun (LMG), which had also appeared in World War I as a means of carrying firepower forward in the assault, had gradually changed its role and in World War II became the "base of fire" for the infantry section. In most armies the basic tactic was the same – the infantry section or squad consisted of ten or a dozen men, two or three of whom were the LMG team (one man to carry and fire the gun, one man to assist him,

A Thompson sub-machine gun advertisement of the 1920s, emphasizing its use by police forces. The exceptionally long barrel was a rarity.

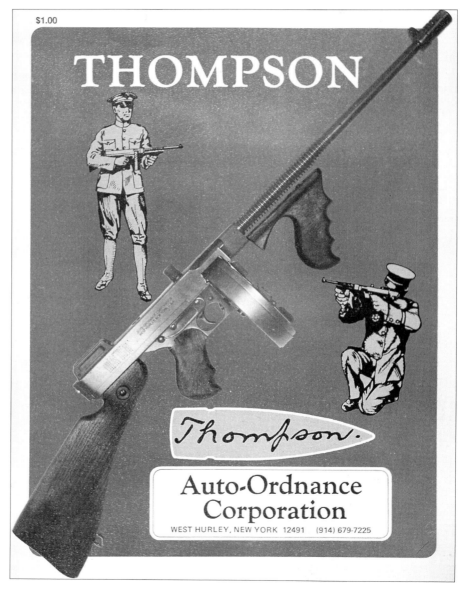

$1.00

THOMPSON

Thompson.

Auto-Ordnance
Corporation
WEST HURLEY, NEW YORK 12491   (914) 679-7225

carry ammunition and change magazines, and possibly a third man with a rifle to give them local protection). On coming under fire during the advance, the entire squad would go to ground and the LMG would open fire in order to keep the enemy's head down, while the riflemen slid off to a flank. There they would take up a position and open fire, giving cover while the LMG section leap-frogged around them to another fire position, where they would take up the covering fire, and thus allow the riflemen to make another move. This alternate movement would continue until they were close enough to charge the enemy position.

All this meant that the LMG became a desirable piece of equipment, and the various armies spent a great deal of time in making their choice. Probably the first to do so were the French who, having had some of the worst machine guns during World War I, were anxious to correct this defect as soon as they could. The Hotchkiss was considered obsolete and beyond improvement, and in any case the Hotchkiss company were more interested in making automobiles in the 1920s than in making weapons. So the job was given to the national arsenal at Chatellerault, and their first move was to design a new cartridge, since the old 8-mm Lebel cartridge was a most inconvenient shape for feeding from an automatic weapon's magazine. The new round was in 7.5-mm caliber and rimless – it appeared in 1924, and shortly afterwards came a LMG, but when the two were tested the results were disastrous. The cartridge was too powerful and there were some defects in the gun, as a result of which a cartridge exploded in the feedway and killed a gunner during a demonstration – end of the 1924 cartridge and gun.

Chatellerault made some changes and in 1929 appeared again with a new cartridge and new gun, and this time they got it right. The gun was gas-operated, firing from a top-mounted 25-round magazine and using a bolt which tipped upwards to jam its rear end into a recess in the receiver to lock the breech. It also had two triggers, one for single shots and the other for automatic fire at 500 rounds per minute. This went into service as the Mle 24/29 and was to be their base of fire until the 1950s.

Britain, of course, had the Lewis gun, but it too was considered some-what elderly, and although one or two inventors had tried to modernize it, the gun was still complicated to manufacture and capable of an amazing variety of stoppages. Something simpler was demanded, and the front-runner was the Vickers-Berthier. Gen Berthier was a French officer who had developed several improvements to the Lebel rifle, and in the 1920s he designed a machine gun – the French army had put their money into the Chatellerault design and were not interested, so Berthier sold it to Vickers in England and they perfected it as the Vickers-Berthier. A simple and robust weapon, it also used gas operation and a tipping bolt, feeding from an overhead curved 30-round magazine. The Indian Army, which, although British-run had a great deal of independence in its choice of weapons,

British troops on the Naktong River in Korea, 1950, with a Bren light machine gun.

accepted it and put it into service in 1933. This acceptance seemed to augur well for British Army acceptance as well, but just as minds were beginning to be made up, the Military Attaché in Prague, Czechoslovakia, reported on a demonstration of a new gun made there, and known simply as the ZB26. His report was so enthusiastic that a gun was bought and tested. It performed so well that minds were rapidly changed. The only snag was that it had been built around the 7.92-mm Mauser cartridge, but the makers, the *Zbrojovka Brno* (or Brno Arms Company), very quickly modified the design to fire the British .303 cartridge – this, among other things, meant shifting the gas port back down the barrel and making the top-mounted magazine curved, so as to accommodate the rimmed .303 round. This performed as flawlessly as the ZB26, and was immediately accepted for British service. It needed a name – the British Army has always disliked numerical codes as names for things – so it became the Bren, using the BR from Brno (its place of origin), and the EN from Enfield, where the Royal Small Arms Factory put it into production in 1937.

Without doubt the Bren is one of the greatest guns ever made, and in this we should also include the original ZB26. It was gas-operated, using a rising bolt which locked into the receiver – an adjustable gas regulator allowed more gas to be tapped off if the gun got sticky with dirt or dust, an adjustable bipod allowed it to be put into action on any sort of ground, there were few parts and a simple mechanism which any soldier could understand and which could be stripped and re-assembled in seconds. It was utterly reliable, amazingly accurate, and robust enough to stand up to virtually anything. The Bren was used by all British and Commonwealth forces except the Indians, who stuck to their Vickers-Berthier. The ZB26 (and a slightly improved later version, the ZB30) was used by the Czechs, Germans, Chinese, Spanish and several other armies, and was copied by the Japanese. And, converted to 7.62-mm NATO caliber, it is still in wide use, notably by the British Army.

Some people didn't get it right – the Italians, for example. They ended World War I with the Fiat medium machine gun and not much else, so that provision of a light machine gun was a fairly high priority. There were two companies capable of making guns, Fiat and Breda, the latter having been thrust into the business by being ordered to make Fiat machine guns during the war. After the war, having acquired a lot of expensive machinery, they decided to keep it and design guns of their own. They did this successfully, so that both they and Fiat made machine guns for the air force. Then came the lucrative contract to outfit the army with a light machine gun – Breda won, so Fiat sold them their gun factory and got out of the business, leaving the former with the monopoly, which wasn't good, because Breda had some funny ideas about machine guns, and coupling these with some funny ideas the army had, produced some odd weapons.

The Breda Model 30 became the standard LMG for the Italian Army – it was an ungainly weapon which must have been the very devil to clean and maintain, and it had one of the oddest feed systems ever seen. It was a blowback gun, loading its ammunition from a permanently fixed magazine on the right-hand side of the gun. This could be released and swung forwards, to expose its mouth, and was then fed on a diet of chargers of 6.5-mm rifle ammunition. The charger was placed in the magazine mouth and the cartridges pushed out, into the magazine. Four five-round chargers filled it, after which the gunner's mate swung it back into place and the gunner fired them off. The theory was that: (a) you saved the cost of thousands of magazines and; (b) you were less likely to damage the feed lips, that part of a detachable magazine which is always the easiest to bend and the most likely source of trouble. The disadvantages were: (a) the rate of fire was slow, since the gunner had to wait while the magazine was being reloaded, and (b) if anything did go wrong with the magazine, then the whole gun was out of the battle. Another design defect was that there was no carrying handle – the gunner had to carry it cradled in his arms – and because there was no carrying handle, when it came time to change the hot barrel, there was nothing to hold it with, so the gunner's mate provided himself with a thick piece of rag or he burned his fingers. And, of course, since it was a blowback weapon using a bottle-necked cartridge case, the ammunition had to be lubricated so that it could be extracted without tearing the empty case to pieces, and this meant having an oil pump inside the gun which sprayed every cartridge with oil on its way into the chamber. This, of course, was found to be a highly inconvenient system when exposed to the desert sands of North Africa.

Breda also made the standard medium (tripod-mounted) machine gun, the Model 37. This fired 8-mm ammunition, and was a very good gun, but again, the feed system was peculiar. The gun had originally been designed for use in tanks, and the Italian Army, quite properly, were apprehensive about empty cartridge cases being ejected inside the tank and perhaps jamming the turret, or otherwise getting into the machinery and causing trouble. Most armies solved this by hanging a bag around the ejection port or, since the gun is usually fixed, running a chute out through a hole in the armor. Not Breda – they devized a mechanism which extracted the cartridge from the metallic feed strip, fired it, extracted the case from the chamber and then replaced it into the feed strip before indexing the strip across and loading the next cartridge. All very well inside a tank, but a nuisance in a field service machine gun where the gunner's mate had to empty the cases out of the feed strip before he could reload it with fresh rounds.

The Japanese also had a few odd ideas. They had originally purchased Hotchkiss guns from France in the 1900s, then built their own copy, but in 1922 they introduced their first native design, the 6.5-mm 11th Year model. Japanese weapons were numbered according to the year of the current emperor's reign, so you have to know which emperor was on the throne at the time, and what his reign was called. In this case it was Emperor Yoshihito, and his period is known as the Taisho era. And the 11th year of his reign was 1922 in the Western calendar. The system was changed in about 1930 to identification by the Japanese year – the last two digits of this differ from the Western year by 60, so that a Type 97 weapon was introduced in 1937, a Type 00 in 1940. The 11th year was another blowback weapon, with the inevitable oil pump, and it fed its ammunition from a hopper on the left-hand side. Into this hopper went chargers of 6.5-mm rifle ammunition, and the mechanism in the hopper stripped away the cartridges from the chargers and fed it, round by round, to the gun. The system had its advantages, in that any rifleman could contribute to the gun in time of need, without having to empty chargers or fill magazines, and it simplified supply because both rifle and light machine gun used exactly the same package of ammunition. But the mechanical arrangements were complicated and easily got out of adjustment, and the gun was prone to stoppages.

In the 1930s it was decided to produce a new gun to replace the 11th Year model, and in 1936 the Type 96 appeared. The oil pump and the hopper were done away with, the feed now being a conventional top-mounted 30-round magazine, but since the mechanism was the same, it still demanded lubricated ammunition, so the oiling was done when the magazine was loaded. It wasn't much of an improvement, and since the Japanese war industry couldn't produce guns fast enough, the 11th Year stayed in service until 1945.

But during their occupation of Manchuria and invasion of northern China in the 1930s, the Japanese encountered the ZB26 gun in the hands of some Chinese units, and this impressed them so much that for their next LMG they copied much of it. This became the Type 99, and it was in a new 7.7-mm caliber – the Sino-Japanese war had shown them that the 6.5-mm round didn't have as much stopping power as the heavier 7.92-mm Mauser favored by the Chinese, but rather than simply adopt the Mauser cartridge, the Japanese designed a completely new round in 7.7-mm caliber. In fact, in one of the most puzzling decisions in firearms history, they adopted three new 7.7-mm cartridges at almost the same time, one rimmed, one rimless and one semi-rimmed. Bearing in mind that, broadly speaking, no gun intended for one of those cartridges can fire any of the others (in fact some guns could fire the rimmed and semi-rimmed, but not very well), that the Japanese rarely head-stamped their cartridges, and that it often needs a micrometer to distinguish a rimless from a semi-rimmed, it makes you wonder why they did it, and what the Japanese supply officers must have had to worry about.

Anyway, they did it, and the Type 99 used the rimless round. The gun was a considerable improvement on what had gone before – the gas-operated locked breech meant that opening could be closely controlled and thus there was a slow and steady extraction phase, so there was no longer any need to oil the cartridges. Reliability improved, accuracy improved, but changing calibers shortly before starting a war with the USA was not the wisest of moves, and the Type 99 never managed to replace the earlier guns throughout the war.

And what of the USA? Well, the US Army had, in the 1930s, put out a request for a light machine gun to fit in between the Browning Automatic Rifle (BAR) and the .30 Browning M1917 medium machine gun. After a good deal of discussion, a specification was drawn up in November 1939 and anybody interested was invited to submit a gun for trials to take place in September 1941.

Several guns appeared from Springfield Arsenal, Auto-Ordnance, Rock Island Arsenal, Colt, Sedgley and Schirgun. None were acceptable, most were too heavy and most belt-fed – of the collection, only the Auto-Ordnance model (designed by a Mr William Ruger, who was to become better known after the war for his pistols) was considered worth further development, but in 1942 there were other more urgent matters to be dealt with, and the LMG programme was shelved.

An American soldier takes aim with his Browning Automatic Rifle in the Philippines, 1944.

By 1943 combat experience indicated that an LMG was needed, and the Auto-Ordnance design was brought out again, given a complete overhaul and redesign, and eventually proved to be an acceptable weapon. But by that time the army, tired of waiting, had taken the standard air-cooled Browning M1919 gun, put a butt and pistol grip on one end, and a bipod and flash hider on the other, and adopted it as the M1919A6 light machine gun. How anybody in his right mind could have considered it light, when it weighed 32 lbs and was 53 inches long (the ZB30, for example, weighed 21 lbs and was 45 inches long) is past belief, but the decision was taken and the LMG programme died, not to be resurrected for many years.

A lot of LMG programmes died in the immediate postwar years, and they died because of a decision the Germans had taken before the war broke out – a decision which turned people's ideas about light and medium machine guns completely upside down. Although the Germans used a number of light machine guns, the ZB26 and ZB30 among them, they were not their preferred type and were often shuffled off to second-line units. In the 1930s the Rheinmetall company had developed what became the MG15, a 7.92-mm aircraft machine gun which was recoil-operated, the barrel and bolt recoiling within the receiver and the bolt being revolved by two rollers riding in cam grooves inside the gun body. The magazine was a "saddle" type holding 75 rounds – it sat across the top of the gun with a drum on each side and fed rounds alternately from each side, so keeping the balance steady as the ammunition was used. The whole gun was laid out in a straight line, the butt being behind the body so that there was no tendency for the gun to rise due to leverage against the firer's shoulder, and there was an ingenious method of changing the barrel in which the butt was rotated and removed, allowing the bolt and barrel to be withdrawn backwards and a new barrel slipped into the jacket. For various technical reasons the air force didn't take to it, so it was given a butt and bipod and the army accepted it as a light machine gun, but in fact it wasn't particularly light and was somewhat cumbersome.

Nevertheless, it had some good features, and the army gave one to the Mauser company and asked them to sort it out. When they had finished with it there was not much left of the original gun except the bolt locking system. The magazine feed was replaced by a belt feed, though by a quick change of the receiver top cover it could be made to accept the 75-round saddle magazine if required. The quick-change barrel was modified by hinging the receiver to the back of the barrel jacket, so that by swinging it to one side the barrel could be removed and changed. And the trigger was made into a double unit whereby pressing the top gave single shots, but pressing the bottom produced automatic fire. The gun, now called the MG34, was built to a high standard, was extremely reliable, weighed 26 lbs, fired at 900 rounds a minute, and the army loved it. And then they had an inspiration. Since it had a very good barrel changing system, there was no reason why, with a couple of spare barrels, the MG34 could keep

A "light" machine gun of World War I, the Maxim 08/15, which substituted the standard tripod-mounted Maxim with a somewhat unstable bipod.

German infantrymen loading an MG34 machine gun during the invasion of France in 1940. The third man, in the background, protects them while the machine gun is temporarily out of action.

up sustained fire, so why not put it on a tripod and make it the support medium machine gun. At the same time, it was light enough, so put a bipod on the front and use it as the squad LMG. Only one machine gun, only one gun for the soldiers to learn, only one gun requiring a supply of spare parts, but one gun capable of doing everything that was needed. In fact, though nobody coined the phrase for many years, they had introduced the General Purpose Machine Gun.

The only trouble was that, looked at critically, the MG34 was too good. It was a complex manufacturing task and it was comparatively expensive – 310RM or about $110. What the army needed, and this became more apparent once the war had begun, was something which could be made a good deal quicker and slightly cheaper if possible, but, of course, without sacrificing reliability or this dual-purpose function. This demand came up in 1941, and when the question was raised with Mauser, they saw that the whole thing revolved around ease of production. So they went to a company specializing in metal pressing and enlisted their aid – their chief engineer got so enthusiastic that he actually went and did the army's machine-gunner course so as to learn at first-hand what the requirements were.

The result was the MG42, and, again, there wasn't a lot left of the MG34 in it. The redesign had gone beyond the skin and changed the system of operation – it was still worked by barrel recoil, but the bolt was now locked to the barrel extension by two rollers which were cammed out into recesses by tracks in the gun body. As barrel and bolt recoiled, so the rollers were moved out until the bolt was free to move under its own momentum. The gun was belt fed, using a very simple mechanism in the top cover of the gun which was driven by the movement of the bolt. The rate of fire – 1,200 rounds a minute – was higher than any previous gun, and the barrel changing was simplified by making a slot in the right rear of the barrel jacket through which the barrel could be quickly withdrawn and replaced. The MG42 was even more reliable than the MG34, and was soon treated with respect by its enemies – the high rate of fire saw to that. Indeed, the high rate of fire made it a little difficult to control on a bipod, but the Germans thought the trouble was worth it. On a tripod it was a superb support gun, and the high firing rate made it an excellent anti-aircraft weapon as well. Over 750,000 were made before the war ended, and after VE-Day, the Allies distributed thousands of them to European countries, thus helping to re-equip their armies. When, in 1954, the revived German Army looked round for a new machine gun they could not find anything as good, in their view, as the MG42, so they simply put it back into production, using the 7.62-mm NATO cartridge. Italy, Austria and Yugoslavia also adopted it, and the MG42 (or, as they now call it, the MG3) looks like going on for a few years yet.

CHAPTER SEVEN

THE HOT COLD WAR

THE GERMAN STURMGEWEHR was first used on the Eastern Front, and, inevitably, one of these new weapons and some ammunition fell into Russian hands. With their own experience of the Federov Automat and its 6.5-mm cartridge, and other experiments they had performed on low-powered cartridges in the 1930s, they immediately saw the significance of the new 7.92-mm short cartridge and the lightweight selective fire rifle that accompanied it, and they very rapidly set about developing a similar cartridge of their own. This appeared in late 1943, a short 7.62-mm round with a 39-mm rimless case, and it was formally adopted as the 7.62-mm M1943 cartridge. Next came the question of developing a suitable rifle, but here there was less urgency, as the Soviets were well-provided with sub-machine guns and standard rifles, and they saw no point in upsetting their production lines to adapt to a totally new cartridge in the middle of a major war, so development was allowed to begin, but it was not given a high priority.

S. G. Simonov had been working away at his rifle design since manufacture of his earlier model stopped in 1939, and he had produced two prototypes of a carbine which showed promise, but which suffered from feed jamming due to the rimmed 7.62-mm cartridge then in use by the Soviets. So Simonov was handed a specimen of the new short 7.62-mm rimless cartridge, and invited to modify his carbine to suit – the rimless round removed all the feed problems and by the middle of 1944 sufficient prototypes had been made to be able to send some to various units in combat to see what they thought of them. As is inevitably the case, combat showed up defects which testing grounds had never even thought of – notably that the Simonov carbine was prone to feed and extraction problems due to dust and dirt.

A member of the US Navy SEALs carrying an M16 rifle with a grenade launcher fitted underneath the barrel, giving him the ability to fire at point targets with bullets or area targets with explosive grenades.

Attention to clearances and one or two other minor modifications were made, and just before the war ended the Simonov design was approved as the SVS-45. In appearance it followed the conventional pattern of rifle, with wooden stock and fore-end, 50 inches long and with a folding bayonet under the barrel. The carbine is gas-operated, the gas piston striking the face of the bolt carrier and driving it back – this first rotates the bolt to unlock it, then opens it to extract and eject the cartridge case. A hammer is cocked as the bolt carrier passes across it, and then the return spring drives the carrier and bolt back again, loading a fresh round and closing and locking the bolt. The Simonov was put into mass-production and widely issued – it was also supplied to other countries in the Communist Bloc such as China and North Korea. But while this was going on, another design was being perfected.

Mikhail Kalashnikov was a railroad clerk who was conscripted into the Soviet Army in 1938 and became a tank driver. When Germany invaded Russia in 1941 he was a sergeant tank commander, and in September of that year he was badly wounded in battle near Bryansk. After his discharge from hospital he was given six months convalescent leave and spent his time designing a sub-machine gun which he submitted to the army. They were impressed, but since it offered no particular advantage over the existing models, turned it down. Nevertheless, there was sufficient evidence of Kalashnikov's talent for him to be sent as a technician to a weapons test establishment, instead of reporting back to the front when his leave expired. Here, he worked for a while on improvements to machine guns, until one day in early 1944 he was given a handful of the new M1943 cartridges and invited to design an assault rifle around them. The rest, as they say, is history.

Kalashnikov's initial design for an assault rifle was submitted in 1946, and what little we know of it suggests that it was a good deal different in appearance from the rifle which finally bore his name. In any event, three years of development followed before, some time in 1949, the *Avtomat Kalashnikov* was approved for service as the AK47, and it was not until some time in 1950 that serious production got under way. Since then there have probably been few days in which the Kalashnikov rifle, in one form or another, has not been in production somewhere in the world.

For Kalashnikov did not merely invent a rifle, he invented a system upon which all sorts of weapons could be constructed – rifles, sub-machine guns, machine guns. They could all be made to work by modifying the basic building blocks of the AK47 rifle. Kalashnikov was not the first man with this idea, nor will he be the last, but he has certainly been the most successful, largely because he had a monolithic dictatorship behind him, a government which simply said "Do this" and it was done. Once the AK47 had been approved for service, Kalashnikov joined the ranks of the successful designers and his ideas carried weight, and when he proposed his system people listened, and when they agreed the job was done.

A Soviet Army recruit
undergoing winter
training, using a
Kalashnikov AK47 rifle.

The first move was to standardize the AK47 in all Communist Bloc
countries – East Germany, Poland, Bulgaria, Romania, Yugoslavia, China,
North Korea. . . the only exception was Czechoslovakia, which had a
thriving arms industry and preferred to use its own design of rifle, though
even so it eventually had to standardize on the 7.62-mm M1943 cartridge. After this, the rifle was supplied to any and every nationalist group
anxious to rise against its rulers, and to any country anxious to provide its
armed forces with modern weapons at a low price. So that, one way or
another, the Kalashnikov spread across the world.

The next move was to adapt the basic design into a light machine gun, which simply meant giving it a heavier barrel, a bipod and a larger magazine. This became the RPK and appeared in the 1950s, after which the PK, a heavier machine gun with a quick-change barrel, belt fed, and firing the rimmed 7.62-mm full-power cartridge, appeared in 1961. Finally the basic mechanism was modified by Dragunov to operate with a short-stroke piston and fire the rimmed cartridge so as to provide a sniping rifle. The Soviet forces were now completely converted to the Kalashnikov system, and the assault rifle had also entirely replaced the sub-machine gun in their armory.

The Russians, of course, were not the only people to have studied the German 7.92-mm short cartridge with interest. Probably the most interested were the British who, even before the war ended, were looking ahead and contemplating a new automatic rifle to replace the elderly Lee-Enfield magazine rifle. The first point to be settled was the cartridge, since the rimmed .303 cartridge was not the ideal for an automatic weapon – at one stage there was a move to adopt the 7.92-mm Mauser cartridge, since this was already in production in Britain for tank machine guns, but contemplation of the German Sturmgewehr and its cartridge soon disposed of that idea. As soon as the war ended an "Ideal Caliber Board" was set up to go closely into the cartridge question, and after much debate and sound reasoning, they arrived at a 7-mm "intermediate" round, shorter than the .303 and somewhat longer than the German short cartridge. It is a notable thing that whenever, and wherever, a commission sits to determine the ideal caliber for an infantry rifle, they always arrive at 7 mm – it is an equally notable thing that nobody ever gets a 7 mm cartridge as a result of it.

Next came the question of a rifle, and a design by Stefan Jansen of the Royal Small Arms Factory at Enfield broke new ground in several directions. Jansen saw the point of having a short cartridge in order to have a compact rifle, but he also appreciated that accuracy and good velocity come from having a long barrel, and he therefore designed his rifle in the fashion known (for unknown reasons) as a "bullpup". In this type of weapon the barrel is the same length as that of a conventional rifle, but the mechanism is set back in the stock so that the shoulder pad is actually at the end of the receiver, instead of being a foot behind it on the end of a piece of wood, and the bolt and chamber are alongside the firer's face. This means that in order to get the trigger in a position convenient to the human form, it is in front of the magazine and chamber by a considerable distance. It also means that the rifle tends to lie low in the firer's grip and that his head, and therefore his eye, is some height above the top of the barrel, which in turn means that the sights have to be lifted up on stalks. Jansen got round this by putting a looped carrying handle on top of the gun and then putting an optical sight on top of the carrying handle at a level to which the eye fell naturally as the rifle was held.

This became the 7-mm Rifle EM2 (for Experimental Model 2), and was a resounding success – it was gas-operated, using hinged flaps to lock the bolt into the receiver and fired from a 20-shot magazine. It was approved for issue in 1951 as the Rifle, 7 mm, No 9 Mark 1, but this announcement merely brought to a head a dispute which had been rumbling through the NATO countries for some months – the question of the future NATO standard cartridge.

Pages could be, and have been, written on this subject, but we can condense it – the British had selected a short cartridge, but the Americans were opposed to it, refusing any reduction in performance from the .30-06 cartridge. The rest of NATO sat around and waited for them to make up their minds. Eventually it became a question of economic clout, and since the Americans were putting up most of the money and equipment for NATO, they had the final say. They were not particularly impressed by the short cartridge argument, but for the sake of amity, agreed to a compromise cartridge, which, in effect, was a .30-06 shortened slightly, but with practically the same performance. By political pressure this was forced on to NATO, and reluctantly agreed by the British, who now had to scrap their rifle and start again.

Fabrique Nationale of Liège had been watching all this from the sidelines and realized, probably before anybody else, which way the wind was blowing. They obtained the dimensions of the compromise cartridge and by the time it was standardized as the 7.62 mm NATO round, they had produced a rifle to suit it. This, of course, didn't happen overnight – Dieudonne Saive, the chief designer for FN, had been working on an automatic rifle for most of the previous 20 years and had a good design almost ready in 1939. He spent the war years in Britain and perfected it, and as soon as the conflict was over, FN went into production with the SAFN 49 to catch the market for automatic rifles. They did this very successfully, selling the SAFN to several nations in various caliber. A gas-operated weapon, semi-automatic only, it was of conventional wood-stocked form and built to a very high standard. As a result it was rather expensive, and Saive set about redesigning it to be easier, cheaper and quicker to make. While he was doing this, the 7.62-mm NATO cartridge dispute rose over the horizon and he rapidly produced a version of his new rifle chambered for the new cartridge.

And being a clever salesmen, Saive offered the rifle to the British – they put it through their usual strenuous trials, approved it in December 1953, ordered 5,000 rifles from Belgium, and for the first time the British Army was outfitted with a rifle designed and developed outside Britain.

The FN FAL (*Fusil Automatique Legere* – light automatic rifle) introduced an entirely new style into rifles. Instead of wooden furniture, stocked to the muzzle, there was a wooden butt and a perforated wooden hand-grip around the barrel and gas cylinder. There was a pistol grip below the receiver and a removable 20-round box magazine. The gas piston, above the barrel, locked and unlocked the bolt by tilting it into recesses in the receiver, and the FAL could be had in either semi-automatic or selective fire versions – most armies took the semi-automatic version, though some, like the Canadian, also took a heavy-barrel selective-fire version and used it as a LMG. Altogether, over 90 armies adopted the FN FAL, almost all in 7.62-mm NATO caliber, and it was also manufactured under license in Britain, Argentina, Austria, Australia, Brazil, India, Israel, Mexico, South Africa and Venezuela.

The Fabrique National FAL rifle, which became standard in over 90 armies around the world.

With a runaway sales success like that going on, you might be excused for thinking that nobody else had much of a chance in the rifle business, but at this same time another design was being born which, eventually, had almost as much success as the FN FAL.

We have noted previously that in the aftermath of World War II there was an exodus of military technicians from Germany to Spain, and a number of small arms engineers and designers were among them. They obtained employment in the Small Arms Technical Centre (CETME) and, having been involved in the development of an assault rifle in the Mauser factory, continued with that project for the benefit of the Spanish. The Mauser Sturmgewehr 45 never got beyond the prototype stage in Germany, but it had adopted a novel breech mechanism which owed something to the MG42 machine gun. This used a breech-block with rollers which were swung outwards by cams into recesses in the receiver to lock the breech closed. In the StuG45 design this was slightly changed so that the rollers were not completely locked, but acted as a retarding device to delay the opening of a blowback breech.

In order to obtain the optimum performance from this new rifle the designers made a package of it, including a completely new 7.92-mm cartridge with a fairly short case and a long, lightweight bullet. This performed very well, but the Spanish were understandably reluctant to change their cartridge without a fairly long investigation – they also felt that it would be useful if they could make a slight profit out of this design, and to that end, since they had no sales organisation of their own, they licensed the design to *Nederland Waapen & Munitiefabrik* (NWM) of Holland. NWM promptly pointed out that the unique cartridge was a sales drawback, and the designers would have to re-jig the weapon to fire a more conventional round.

In 1956 NWM interested the German Army in the new rifle, and, as NWM had forecast, they wanted it chambered for the 7.62-mm NATO cartridge. CETME provided 400 rifles and the Germans gave them a very thorough test in competition with the FN-FAL. Generally, they liked the rifle, but felt that it could do with some improvement, and passed the job to another company, Heckler & Koch of Oberndorf, Germany. Basically the problem was that CETME had designed the rifle to be cheaply manufactured without the need for precise tolerances and expensive machining, but this was allied to the original cartridge – loaded with the 7.62-mm NATO round, which was more powerful, this sort of manufacture would not do, and Heckler & Koch had to re-design the rifle to improve the tolerances and include heavier metal and more complex construction.

The result was the Gewehr 3 (or G3), which was adopted by the German Army in 1959 and is still their principal weapon. It has also been adopted by 50 or more other armies and is, or has been, made under license in 12 countries ranging from France to Myanmar. It proved particularly

The German G3 rifle,
which more or less
armed those armies of
the free world which
didn't adopt the FN-
FAL. It uses a roller-
delayed blowback
system with great
success.

popular in Africa and South America, and became the standard of such major forces as the Pakistan and Turkish armies.

The G3 relies on a two-part breech bolt, the front part carrying a pair of rollers, while the rear part carries the firing pin assembly. As the bolt closes behind the cartridge, the front part stops, but the rear part continues to move and forces the two rollers out into recesses. On firing, the cartridge case pressure on the face of the bolt is transferred to the rear section of the bolt, and this has to move back first so that the rollers can be squeezed back out of the recesses before the breech can open. This gives a sufficient amount of delay to allow the bullet to clear the muzzle and the chamber pressure to drop to safe limits, so that the usual problems with bottle-necked cases and blowback operation – lubricated ammunition or grooved chambers – are avoided. The basic design proved so successful that it was adjusted to suit the 7.62 x 39 mm M1943 Soviet cartridge, in the hope of tempting various countries which had adopted the AK47 rifle and its cartridge, but whose allegiance to the Soviets was wavering, but so far as we know there were few takers. But by the early 1960s there was another cartridge beginning to make its presence felt.

After 1945 the US Army tested a number of experimental rifles and eventually settled on an improved Garand known as the M14. This, in effect, replaced the Garand's eight-round clip magazine system with a removable 20-round box magazine, changed the caliber to 7.62-mm NATO, and gave the rifle a full-automatic fire capability. In fact, this latter facility was soon removed or put out of action, since firing such a powerful cartridge from this rifle proved it to be uncontrollable in automatic fire. At much the same time the army had set up an Operations Research Office (ORO) to apply scientific study and analysis to various military problems, and this, during the Korean War in 1952, began studying body armor for infantry troops. To make any sensible assessment of body armor meant first studying the frequency and location of wounds sustained by soldiers, and after a massive analysis of some three million casualty reports, some surprising conclusions emerged.

The ORO investigation showed that hits on the human body were randomly distributed, whether or not they came from aimed fire, random fire or splinters from grenades or artillery shells. In other words, a man in combat was no more likely to be wounded by a properly aimed rifle bullet than he was likely to be wounded by a casual shell splinter. They also rediscovered what the Germans had found in the 1930s – that most of the rifle fire in warfare takes place at ranges under 300 metres, and that there was thus no justification for hanging on to a powerful rifle cartridge capable of killing out to ranges of 2,000 metres. It was a pity that they had not reached these conclusions before the 7.62-mm NATO cartridge was developed.

We need not dwell too long on the various theories put forward, except to say that one popular solution appeared to be to fire a number of small projectiles in a cluster in the general direction of the enemy, so that there was an improved chance of at least one of the cluster striking him. From this came studies which showed that a small bullet could be as disabling as a large one, and that the recoil impulse from a small bullet would be low, thus permitting such bullets to be fired at automatic rates without losing control of the rifle.

This led to a decision to develop a .22 caliber (5.56 mm) military rifle. The Remington company had a .222 centre-fire sporting cartridge in production, and this was used for some experiments, after which the army asked the ArmaLite Division of the Fairchild Airplane & Engine Company to develop a rifle. ArmaLite had come into existence in 1954 because Richard Boutelle, the president of Fairchild, had been attracted by the theories of one George Sullivan, a patent attorney who had some ideas about using modern synthetics and alloys to produce lightweight weapons. The division also attracted Eugene Stoner (a man who had been designing rifles since retiring from military service), and his design team set about developing a lightweight military rifle. They produced the AR-10 rifle in 7.62 mm caliber in 1956, but by that time the FN-FAL had gone into production and the AR-10 was not sufficiently developed to compete with it. But, since the AR-10 had impressed the army by virtue of its original design, in 1957 ArmaLite were asked to develop a 5.56-mm weapon with a 20-shot magazine and weighing six pounds or less, capable of piercing a standard steel helmet at 500 yards range. To achieve this last demand meant modifying the .222 Remington cartridge to obtain more velocity, and Stoner expanded the case capacity so that eventually the rifle was able to fire a 55 grain bullet at 3,300 ft per second. The new cartridge became the .223 Remington and, later, the 5.56-mm NATO round.

Stoner's new rifle was the AR-15 – it used light alloys and plastics, had a rotating bolt in a bolt carrier, a carrying handle which also carried the sights high above the barrel axis, necessary because the rifle was almost a straight-line design so that there was less leverage about the butt to cause the muzzle to rise when firing automatic. A number of prototypes were delivered to the army for testing, and, in general, the army was impressed enough to demand further development. Long arguments between various military factions and ArmaLite then followed, the upshot of which was that Fairchild sold the rights in the rifle to Colt who, wearying of attempts to convince the army, managed to sell 8,500 rifles to the US Air Force for use by airfield guards. In this role it appeared in Vietnam in 1962 – the South Vietnamese found it better suited to their men than the M14 rifle and began adopting it. From there it spread to the US Army in Vietnam, and by the middle 1960s, the 5.56-mm rifle – now called the M16 – became the US standard infantry rifle.

This, of course, made nonsense of NATO standardisation – one major army now used 5.56 mm for its rifle, while the remainder used 7.62 mm. The gunmakers looked at the situation and decided that 5.56 mm was the coming caliber and began developing rifles and machine guns, while the armies and their governments sat back and made up their minds about what they were going to do.

The root of the problem lay in the varying opinions of the worth of the 5.56-mm bullet. A favorite demonstration of the 5.56 mm party at this time was to fire two rifles, one 5.56 mm and one 7.62 mm, at two one-gallon cans filled with water. The 7.62 mm bullet went straight through both sides of the can, leaving two spurts of water coming from front and back. The 5.56 mm made a neat hole going in, after which the can simply exploded, the back being blown violently open and the entire contents dispersed in spray. In warmer countries the demonstration was usually done with a melon or pumpkin, with similar results. This, it was maintained, showed that while the 7.62 mm merely drilled its way through the opposition, the 5.56 mm was "inherently unstable" and as soon as it struck any solid object the bullet would tumble and thus "deliver up all its kinetic energy to the target". The instability was due to the bullet being spun at something less than the optimum rate, so that striking any obstacle would easily deflect it from its path and allow it to broadside. All sorts of wild stories circulated about the amazing killing power of the 5.56-mm bullet; a man was struck on the forearm and a shock wave ran down his main artery and paralysed his heart, and so forth. At that time the study of wound ballistics was not so voluminous as to be able to refute these theories, and as a result the weapon acquired a sinister reputation which the peace parties were not slow to embroider. In later years it was shown that much of this theory was untrue, and that bullet construction and other factors had a considerable bearing on the wounding power of rifles – moreover, the experience of soldiers with both calibers of rifle in action have tended to show that while the 5.56 mm is a satisfactory bullet for wounding, it is less satisfactory for stopping an advancing man, and there is still a very large body of opinion which argues that the 5.56-mm bullet, for all its casualty-producing capability, simply lacks authority on the battlefield.

But in the early 1960s the mystique of the 5.56-mm bullet held good, and people were even going to smaller calibers in an endeavour to give the soldier as much ammunition per pound as he could possibly want. Calibers as small as 0.17 of an inch (4.3 mm) were tried out, but none of them stayed the course since none of them had sufficient power to defeat steel helmets at reasonable fighting ranges, and most of them were sadly lacking in repeatable accuracy.

As we have already noted, the US Army had begun various experiments under the ORO, and these now left that organisation and were being conducted by the army. From them came *Project Salvo*, and several other small-arms projects, all seeking to improve the chance of the soldier hitting his target, though without actually having to go to the trouble of training the soldier to shoot properly. By this time the infantry soldier was being showered with equipment – grenades, mortars, rocket launchers, radios, position-finders, machine guns, sub-machine guns – all of which demanded training time, and the more new and glamorous the item, the more training time it got, until the rifle, and how to shoot it, slipped a long way down the list of priorities. *Project Salvo* argued that firing a number of projectiles in a controlled burst of fire, or as sub-projectiles of a single cartridge, would improve the chance of hitting – if the aim was slightly off the target, then the dispersion of the projectiles would ensure that at least one of them should hit. Various solutions, such as cartridges with two or three bullets inside them, cartridges firing a number of "flechettes" – inch-long arrows – were tried, but the most promising solution, and certainly the easiest, appeared to be to provide the rifle with a pre-set facility which would permit a three-round burst of fire for a single pull of the trigger. Assuming the first round went where the rifle was aimed, should it near-miss, then the other two rounds, randomly dispersed about the trajectory of the first round, would probably hit. Rifles with "three-round burst fire" settings began to appear.

But, as with the assault rifle, it was the German Army which did its homework hardest and specified the ultimate solution. In 1969 the army gave contracts to three companies – Diehl, Heckler & Koch and IWKA – giving them a fairly free hand to develop an infantry weapon with a better hit probability than anything then in existence, capable of piercing a steel helmet at 500 metres and of automatic fire. Diehl and IWKA soon fell out of the race, because they could see no way of obtaining the desired performance without some radical new technology. Heckler & Koch, on the other hand, had been doing some work on the possibility of a caseless cartridge, and they saw that this was the only solution to the problem which was the principal stumbling block. This problem was simply that the defect of the three-round burst rifle had been exposed – the first round always went where the rifleman pointed it, the second round went about a foot higher

The US M16 rifle
accompanied by the
M249 Squad Automatic
Weapon, also known as
the FN Minimi light
machine gun.

because the rifle was rising under the recoil of the first round, and the third round went skyward because by that time the recoil of two rounds had lifted the muzzle well above the horizon. And the mathematicians showed that only by firing those three rounds at a rate of 2,000 rounds per minute would it be possible to get all three of them into the region of the target before the muzzle lifted. And no conventional rifle could fire, extract, reload and fire again at 2,000 rounds per minute. So if a conventional rifle could not do the job, then an unconventional rifle had to be invented, and Heckler & Koch set to work to design one around a caseless cartridge.

The idea of the caseless cartridge had been put forward a number of times in the past. The ordinary metal-cased cartridge has a number of advantages for the designer which are, perhaps, not readily apparent. In the first place it holds the bullet, the propellant powder and the cap in a nice compact, safe, and reasonably waterproof unit. The case expands on firing to fit tightly in the chamber and seal against any escape of gas rearward, and then contracts rapidly when the pressure drops so that it can be extracted and ejected. The brass (or steel in some cases) of the case acts as a "heat sink", absorbing some of the intense heat of the explosion, and thus preventing the metal of the gun from getting too hot. But there are also some disadvantages – the brass case makes up a considerable amount of the weight of the cartridge, and it has to be removed from the chamber and got rid of before the next round can be loaded. By doing away with the case, and making the cartridge out of a solid lump of propellant, with the bullet embedded in one end and a combustible cap in the other, the complete round would be lighter, therefore allowing the soldier to carry more ammunition for the same weight, and there would be nothing to extract once it was fired so that reloading could commence immediately the breech was opened. Against this was the need to devise some form of making the breech closure gas-tight and, the most important and difficult, getting rid of the heat which would now be directly absorbed by the chamber. The significance of this was that a round loaded into a very hot chamber will often "cook off" – fire itself by the influence of the heat of the chamber igniting the propellant.

While Heckler & Koch were drawing up designs on paper and making experiments, a significant new design of rifle made its appearance in Austria. The Austrian Army needed a modern rifle, and for various reasons connected with their peculiar peace treaty and state of neutrality, it was politically advisable for them to produce it themselves, rather than buy an existing design such as the FN-FAL or the G3. This would cause no problem, since Austria contained the Steyr-Mannlicher factory which had been making military arms for a century or so, and knew their business. The Austrian Army decided they wanted a 5.56-mm weapon, and Steyr drew up a design they called the *Armee Universal Gewehr*, or AUG, a weapon which looked like no other gun the world had ever seen before.

The Steyr-Mannlicher AUG rifle is built on a modular system which allows it to be changed to fit whatever role you need filled; in this case it has been modified into a 9-mm sub-machine gun by changing barrel, bolt and magazine housing.

The AUG was built into a plastic casing in such a way that the various parts could be interchanged – the barrel was available in four lengths and weights so that it could be put together as a sub-machine gun, a carbine, a rifle or a light machine gun. The receiver was built with a carrying handle containing an optical sight, but if an adjustable telescopic sight was preferred, then a replacement receiver carried a simple flat sight mount on to which any telescope or night sight could be fitted. The firing mechanism, inside the butt (because this was a "bullpup" rifle) permitted single shots or automatic fire, but it could be replaced by alternative mechanisms allowing single shots only, or three-round bursts, or any combination of the possibles – hence the word "Universal" in the title. It was actually "modular" in its construction, and by changing "modules" you could come up with precisely the weapon you wanted. The AUG was adopted by the Austrian Army in the early 1970s, and had since gone on to arm several more forces, notably the Australian and New Zealand armies and several in the Middle East.

But what caught the eye in the AUG was the enveloping plastic body, and Heckler & Koch saw that this approach would allow them to produce a weapon which allowed movement to go on inside the body and yet be protected from dust and dirt. In 1979 NATO decided on a long and complex series of trials to settle the question of the next NATO standard small arms cartridge – the various NATO countries were invited to submit rifles and cartridges, and among them was the G11 rifle from Heckler and Koch firing a 4.7-mm caseless cartridge.

The G11 is undoubtedly one of the most brilliant designs of this century, and it solved the seemingly unsolvable problem in a practical fashion. The entire mechanism of the rifle "floats" inside a rifle-shaped plastic casing. The magazine lies along the top of the barrel and feeds straight down into the breech. The breech is a rotating disc, in the edge of which is the chamber, and this disc is rotated by a gas piston or, in initially loading the rifle, by a twist-handle on the side of the casing. To load, the soldier slides the magazine in and twists the handle – the disc rotates to bring the chamber facing upwards, a caseless cartridge drops in from the magazine, and the disc rotates back so that the chamber lies behind the barrel. The trigger is pulled and a firing pin hits the cap, the propellant explodes and the bullet departs. The entire mechanism of barrel and breech recoils inside the outer plastic casing, a gas piston rotates the disc, a round drops in and the disc turns back. The mechanism is returned by a return spring and the rifle is reloaded. So much for single shots. Automatic fire works the same way, except that there is no pause between the breech closing and the firing pin going forward to fire the round. Automatic fire takes place at a rate of about 600 rounds per minute.

It is in the mechanics of the three-round burst that the design leaves the conventional and reaches into a new dimension. It will be recalled that the theory showed that a rate of 2,000 rounds per minute was needed to achieve the desired hit probability, and this rate is achieved by abandoning the usual method of firing. On pressing the trigger for a three-round burst the round in the chamber is fired, the mechanism begins to recoil inside the casing and during that movement the breech is opened and reloaded, closed and fired for the second shot. The recoil movement continues, now intensified by the addition of the recoil force of the second shot, and the breech is again opened, reloaded, closed and fired. The third round's recoil force is now added and an extra-long travel is permitted to the mechanism, which now comes to rest and the recoil blow is transferred to the casing and thus to the firer's shoulder – long after the third bullet has left the barrel. The breech now reloads for a fourth time and returns to the forward position, with the rifle loaded and cocked. The actual rate of fire of those three shots is about 2,200 rounds per minute, and the noise is a prolonged explosion rather than three distinct reports. And the three rounds all land within about a foot of each other at 200 yards range.

It would be nice to record that the G11 outshot all contenders and became the new NATO rifle, but real life is rarely like that and, in fact, the rifle had to be withdrawn from the trial because of the prime defect we have already mentioned – "cooking off" the rounds when loaded into a hot chamber. Heckler & Koch, together with Dynamit Nobel (the ammunition experts), thought about this for a while and then redesigned the cartridge. The original cartridge used a conventional nitro-cellulose propellant, plasticized and moulded around the bullet, and this propellant had an ignition point which was below the temperature achieved by a hot chamber after prolonged firing. The solution was to adopt an entirely new kind of propellant –

The most innovative weapon of the century, the Heckler & Koch G11 rifle, using a caseless cartridge. The magazine lies on top of the barrel area, feeding downwards into a rotary breech block. The rotary cocking handle can be seen on the side.

a de-natured high explosive compound, which produced the ballistic results required, but had an ignition temperature about 100°C higher than that of nitro-cellulose, and well above the temperature reached by a hot chamber.

By that time the NATO trial was over, and the 5.56-mm cartridge, though with a slightly heavier bullet than the original American round, had been agreed upon as the new NATO standard infantry rifle round. Nevertheless, the Germans still considered that their caseless solution was the right answer, and while they were happy to stay with the 7.62-mm NATO round for their machine guns and other weapons, so far as the infantry assault rifle was concerned, it would be the 4.7-mm G11. Plans were laid, contracts signed, and 1990 set as the date for the introduction of the new rifle. The rest of the 1980s was devoted to overhauling the design, reducing the number of parts and generally perfecting it.

Then, of course, fate intervened – the Berlin Wall came down, East and West Germany were re-united, and the Federal German government found itself in desperate need of money to refurbish the newly acquired territory of East Germany. And since the danger of the Soviet Army over-running West Germany now appeared to have receded, the obvious place to get money was from the defense budget. The G11 contract was among the first to be cancelled – about 1,000 rifles had been issued to German special forces, but after that the production lines were stopped, and that was that. It drove Heckler & Koch into bankruptcy, from which they were rescued by British Aerospace and absorbed within the British Royal Ordnance organisation.

Before that happened, though, they had one last run for their money when the US Army decided, in 1982, to look ahead and plan for their next generation assault rifle. They were attracted by the caseless solution and issued contracts to Heckler & Koch and to the AAI Corporation to develop suitable weapons. Some time after that they decided that, in order to cover all the possible options, they would ask other manufacturers for a non-caseless solution – the principal concern was to make sure that after making a final decision somebody would not appear from the undergrowth with a design they had not considered. So the Steyr-Mannlicher, Colt, AAI, McDonnell Douglas and Ares companies all received development contracts. The specification was simple – improve upon the hit probability of the M16A2 rifle by 100 percent at all ranges up to 600 metres.

The resulting rifles appeared for trial in 1989. Four designs were produced, McDonnell Douglas and Ares having fallen by the wayside. The Colt was an improved M16 firing a double-bullet cartridge; the Heckler & Koch was the G11 with some cosmetic changes; the Steyr-Mannlicher fired a flechette from a plastic cartridge and used a novel rising chamber to load and fire the round; and the AAI design has never been fully divulged, but is believed to have had three chambers in a moving sector which fired them in rapid succession. None of them achieved the desired degree of improvement and the Advanced Combat Rifle programme was closed down, having cost the American taxpayer something in the order or $300 million.

The conclusion to be drawn from that expensive programme – and from others which we need not examine – is that the design of the military rifle has got about as far as it can go within the bounds of economic sense. The efficiency, reliability and accuracy of present-day rifles is everything that can be desired – every military rifle is capable of better results than the average soldier can extract from it. Every nuance of gas operation, recoil operation, cartridge and bullet design and propellant and sighting technology has been studied inside and out, and is thoroughly understood. There is no way that any significant improvement can be made in rifle design without an enormous expenditure of time and money and, most significantly, some technological innovation which, at present, cannot be imagined. And if these requirements are met, the cost of the development and production of such a new weapon would be enormous, and the probable improvement in performance would be derisive in comparison to the cost. There is a rule of thumb in the missile business that says "The final ten percent of performance is sixty percent of the development cost" and the same rule now applies to rifles.

With regard to other classes of weapon, the limit may not yet have been reached. The sub-machine gun came out of World War II having, as it were, come of age as far as its tactical use was concerned, but the weapons with which most armies finished the war – the Sten, for example – were scarcely at the forefront of technology, having been hastily developed for wartime use and cheap manufacture. There was room for improvement and several manufacturers set about the task, sure that there would be a market for a well-built sub-machine gun. The first significant technical advance came from Czechoslovakia with the CZ23 family of guns – there were four weapons, the CZ23, 24, 25 and 26 which were all the same

The Czechoslovakian CZ25 sub-machine gun introduced the concept of the "telescoping bolt", which partly surrounds the barrel making it a more compact weapon.

except that the odd-numbered ones fired the 9-mm Parabellum cartridge and the even-numbered ones the 7.62-mm Soviet pistol cartridge, the 23 and 24 had wooden stocks and the 25 and 26 had folding stocks. What they all had in common was an "overhung" or "telescoping" bolt.

In the earlier sub-machine guns the design was ruled by the need to have a heavy bolt and give it enough room to be blown back a sufficient distance to lose some momentum and be arrested by some sort of spring or buffer. This governed the length of the receiver behind the breech. In the CZ design the barrel entered the receiver and was unsupported for some distance around the chamber area, while the bolt was hollowed out in front so that the actual face of the breech was well inside the bolt. When the bolt closed, therefore, the hollow part enveloped the rear end of the barrel. This meant that a good deal of the weight of the bolt was actually in front of the chamber and bolt face, and thus the amount of space behind the bolt, to allow for its recoil, could be shortened, giving a shorter overall length for the weapon. Slots in the bolt allowed for loading and ejection of the spent case. The design also meant that the chamber could be positioned so that the magazine could be slid into the pistol grip, like a pistol magazine. This has two advantages – in the first place it puts the weight at the centre of balance so that the balance of the weapon changes little as the magazine is emptied, and, secondly, when it comes to changing magazines in the dark, it is much easier because "hand finds hand", and if you know that the magazine has to go inside the hand wrapped around the grip you can place it much more surely than if you are trying to find a magazine housing at some unidentified place ahead of your hand in the darkness.

During the first Arab-Israeli War of 1948 the Israelis found themselves short of reliable sub-machine guns, and as soon as the war was over Maj Uziel Gal of the Israeli Defense Force set about designing one. Numbers of CZ23 type guns had appeared in Israel – they were purchasing weapons wherever they could at that time – and the advantages of the overhung bolt were apparent to him. He therefore developed a very similar weapon, but made it even more compact by using the advanced primer ignition system of the Sten gun, in which the cartridge fires before the bolt has come to a stop. This allowed a further reduction in bolt weight and travel. The Uzi sub-machine gun was designed to a high standard of manufacture and finish, and particular attention was paid to designing it so that sand and dust would be expelled from the mechanism rather than retained so as to clog it. The gun went into production in 1951 and rapidly gained a high reputation – production was licensed to *Fabrique Nationale* in Belgium, who supplied it to the West German Army, and production guns from Israel were supplied to several other armies in various parts of the world. Its compact dimensions also led to it being adopted by a number of police forces and similar agencies.

The Heckler & Koch company, having made a success of their G3 rifle, decided to apply the same delayed blowback system to other weapons – they made a number of light machine guns which were basically G3 rifles with heavier barrels, belt or magazine feed, and sundry other accessories, and then they turned to a sub-machine gun. The result was the MP5 (Machine Pistol 5), and because of its unique system of operation – taken from the rifle – this weapon has one considerable advantage over almost every other sub-machine gun, in that it fires from a closed bolt. With most sub-machine guns, and some light machine guns, the weapon is cocked by pulling back the bolt until it is held by the trigger mechanism. When the trigger is pulled, the bolt runs forward, chambers the first round and fires it, after which the gun continues to fire so long as the trigger remains pressed and there is ammunition in the feedway. This is "firing from an open bolt", and it has the advantage that when the trigger is released, the bolt is held again in the open position and air can circulate through the empty barrel and cool it down before the next shot.

With the MP5, the weapon is cocked by pulling back the bolt and releasing it, whereupon it closes on the loaded chamber, leaving a hammer cocked. Pressing the trigger releases the hammer to fire the round. Releasing the trigger allows the bolt to close, loading another round, but leaves the hammer cocked. This is "firing from a closed bolt". It does not permit the cooling flow of air, but in a rifle this is of no importance – in an automatic weapon it can be important, but is perhaps less vital in a sub-machine gun, where short bursts are the rule and there is never any sustained fire to really warm the barrel to a hazardous degree. What is advantageous about the closed bolt system is that when the trigger is pressed, only the hammer moves – in an open bolt weapon the entire bolt runs several inches forward in the gun, and this can cause a significant shift of balance and thus of the aim, between pulling the trigger and having the gun go off. Which means that a gun firing

The Israeli Uzi sub-machine gun has elements of the CZ design in it. It can also be found with a wooden butt, and smaller models – the Mini-Uzi and Micro-Uzi are also available.

Favorite weapon of Special Forces all over the world is the Heckler & Koch MP5 sub-machine gun. Its reliability and first-shot accuracy make it "the one to beat" in any sub-machine gun contest.

from a closed bolt is a good deal more likely to put its first shot where the firer aimed it than is an open bolt weapon. This in itself is sufficient to commend the MP5 to special forces units, who demand accuracy from that first shot – in dealing with a sentry, for example – and thus the MP5 has become the preferred weapon for such units as the British Special Air Service, the US Navy SEALS and the German GSG9.

The rise of the assault rifle spelled the decline of the sub-machine gun in military hands. The sub-machine gun was originally chosen because it was more compact than the contemporary rifle, but once the rifle became more compact, with folding stocks and short barrels, there was little to choose between them so far as weight and dimensions were concerned, and in many armies the assault rifle completely replaced the sub-machine gun. The Soviets were the first to make the change, and after the arrival of the Kalashnikov rifle the PPS and PPSh weapons did not last long – indeed, in Soviet nomenclature the AK47 was classed as a sub-machine gun and not as a rifle. The American M3 sub-machine gun has almost vanished, its place taken by the M16 rifle, and the French Army has replaced their sub-machine guns entirely by the FAMAS 5.56 mm assault rifle.

On the other hand, there are military occupations where an assault rifle is hardly the optimum choice for a weapon – a truck driver, for example, may possibly be called upon to protect himself in an ambush by guerrilla parties on the line of supply. In such a case a sub-machine gun would make more sense than a rifle, and it was this sort of reasoning which led some rifle makers to modify their designs into sub-machine guns. The 5.56-mm Steyr AUG, for example, can be changed into a 9-mm sub-machine gun by exchanging the barrel and bolt and placing an adapter in the magazine housing. The M16 rifle has been redesigned into a 9-mm sub-machine gun configuration. Such conversions are liked by the military mind because if they are based on rifles already in service, they reduce the amount of training time required – once the basic weapon is understood, it doesn't matter whether it is handed to the soldier in 5.56-mm or 9-mm form. It works much the same way.

Another approach was to develop special shortened versions of the assault rifle for filling the sub-machine gun slot, but these were less successful, since the basic rifle upon which the design rested had been developed to fire a specific cartridge in a specific length of barrel, and firing the same cartridge in a much shorter barrel often produces inaccuracy, excessive flash and blast, and even the ejection of unburned powder from the muzzle, because the designed combustion of the powder cannot take place in a barrel which is too short. The Soviets discovered this when they shortened the Kalashnikov rifle to produce the AKSU sub-machine gun for use by drivers, and they had to put an expansion chamber at the front end of the barrel to reduce the blast and flash, ensure complete combustion of the powder, and reduce the violence of the gas action.

Economics come into this as well – assault rifles are not cheap, even in the quantities in which armies buy them. And in the late 1980s, *Fabrique*

US Navy SEALs wading ashore with M16 rifles fitted with grenade launchers.

National of Belgium considered this matter and realized that in any army, only about 20 percent of the men actually need an assault rifle. The other 80 percent would be quite satisfied with a cheaper, shorter-range self-defense weapon which would meet all their requirements. This would also have the advantage of placing the choice of assault rifle solely in the hands of the infantry who were going to use it, instead of making it a weapon acceptable to the entire army, as happens today.

The sub-machine gun was not the answer, since it fired pistol ammunition and had a relatively short range, poor accuracy at longer ranges and a serious lack of penetrative power at any range over about 50 yards. *Fabrique Nationale* envisaged a light and handy weapon, but one which would have a range of 200–250 yards and sufficient power to defeat body armor and steel helmets at that range. Not only were they going to have to design a weapon – it was fairly obvious that they would have to start by designing a cartridge that would do what they wanted.

The result of this appeared in 1990 as the FN P90, and it ushered in a new class of firearm – the Personal Defense Weapon or PDW. It was, in effect, a sub-machine gun, but it differed from its predecessors by not using a pistol cartridge. Instead it used a newly designed 5.7-mm bottle-necked

The original Personal Defense Weapon concept: the 5.7 mm Fabrique National P90 with its unique ammunition.

The object of the P90 is to arm that 80 percent of an army which only needs self-defense weapons, such as this soldier who shows how conveniently the weapon can be carried at the ready even when driving a truck.

cartridge with a composite plastic/metal bullet which was capable of penetrating 48 layers of Kevlar (the synthetic material from which body armor is woven) at over 50 metres range, and a standard US steel helmet at 150 metres. The bullet has three times the stopping power of the 9-mm Parabellum, and does not disintegrate when it strikes the body. The weapon itself uses a plastic casing into which the metal components fit, in parallel with the AUG and G11 rifles, is a blowback weapon firing from a closed bolt, and has the magazine laid along the top of the receiver, the cartridges lying across the longer axis of the gun and rotated by a turntable device so as to fall into the feedway. It is an odd-looking weapon, but one which falls into the hands readily as soon as you pick it up, and which is easy and comfortable to fire with accuracy.

The appearance of the P90 has led to other people taking an interest in this PDW idea – there is every likelihood than the 5.7-mm cartridge will shortly be NATO-standardized, and certainly the British, French and German armies are all examining the PDW concept with a view to reducing their requirement for expensive assault rifles.

Machine guns are another area with scope for development. For example, the .50 Browning, which has dominated the non-Soviet section of the world for almost 70 years, has now been outclassed by the light armored vehicles which abound on today's battlefield. From time to time the ammunition has been improved, but the point has now been reached where there is no more room for improvement, and it is now arguable that a replacement weapon should be developed. The Russians, and their erstwhile customers, have a powerful 14.5-mm weapon at their disposal, but there is nothing comparable with this in the west. There was – *Fabrique Nationale* developed a potent 15-mm machine gun in the 1980s, a weapon which totally outperformed both the Browning and the 14.5 mm Russian weapon, but there was surprisingly little interest shown by the world, and when financial problems beset FN they elected to put the BRG-15 machine gun to one side and concentrate their energies on the P90 PDW described previously. Now that the P90 appears to have been successfully launched, perhaps the BRG-15 will be taken from the shelf, dusted off and placed in the showcase.

The other great question in the machine gun world has been whether or not to adopt the 5.56-mm cartridge as a machine gun standard. Generally speaking, if the infantry rifle of the army is a 5.56-mm weapon, then it has to automatically follow that the LMG will also be a 5.56-mm weapon, otherwise the interchange of ammunition between rifle and LMG is impossible, and a dangerous logistical problem raises its head. But the design and development of 5.56-mm machine guns has not been without its rough spots. While the pure mechanical questions of design were relatively simple – either scaling down a successful 7.62-mm mechanism or beefing-up a successful 5.56-mm rifle design – a strange phenomenon appeared in the early days of development. The machine gun's barrel was usually worn beyond the point of accuracy within 5,000 rounds or so, and this was hardly an economic figure. At one stage it seemed as if there was a point at which the reduction in caliber and the increase in velocity and rate of fire all came together in a disastrous combination which wore out barrels at a nightmarish speed. But careful analysis of the problem, followed by careful design so as to keep the rate of fire at a figure which precluded overheating, quick-change barrels, good cooling arrangements and perhaps some adjustment of the national preference in propellant powder, have brought the barrel life to a figure which is acceptable.

The concept of the General Purpose Machine Gun (GPMG), developed by the Germans with their MG34 and MG42 designs, was avidly grasped by most of the rest of the world after 1945. The British abandoned the Vickers and adopted the Belgian FN MAG design, though they retained the Bren in 7.62-mm caliber; the Americans abandoned the Browning and the BAR and adopted a new belt-fed, gas-operated gun in the M60; the French abandoned the Chatellerault and the heavy Hotchkiss and adopted the AAT-52, a delayed blowback belt-fed weapon.

The Soviets, not bound by normal economic rules, kept everything and superimposed the Kalashnikov PK series of machine guns as their General Purpose design. The West German army simply put the MG42 back into production, calling it the MG3.

By the 1970s several armies were beginning to have second thoughts about the GPMG theory – it worked well enough in the context of a major European war, but in brush-fire wars and small engagements it was less happy. The infantry section were carrying a somewhat cumbersome belt-fed weapon, and felt that something lighter and magazine-fed might do the job just as well. The British, who had retained their wartime Bren, were perhaps less affected by this, but other forces felt the need for a lighter weapon, and the introduction of the 5.56-mm caliber was the final push needed to bring about the change.

FN of Belgium, never slow to see a trend developing, were early in the field with a 5.56-mm LMG, known as the Minimi. A gas-operated weapon of conventional type, it had one novel feature – the fact that it would feed equally well from either a belt or a box magazine of the M16

The Fabrique National Minimi light machine gun in 5.56-mm caliber, is shown here prepared for belt feeding. By removing the belt and flipping the cover over the belt port, a port for inserting a rifle magazine is exposed and ready for immediate use.

**The Minimi is light
enough to be fired from
the shoulder like a rifle.**

rifle pattern, without the need for any adjustment or parts-changing. All that was needed was to move a hinged cover from one aperture to another and insert the appropriate feeding device – the bolt was designed to feed from either position with equal facility. Indeed, the company was, if anything, a little too quick "out the traps", and produced the Minimi before most armies saw the need for it, and it was to take several years before it made its mark.

Shortly after the Minimi had appeared, another 5.56-mm design arrived from a totally unexpected quarter – Chartered Industries of Singapore. This firm had been set up to manufacture the M16 rifle under licence for supply to the Singapore armed forces, and it then went on to develop a 5.56-mm rifle of its own design. Then in the early 1980s it produced the Ultimax LMG, which was somewhat unusual in employing a 100-round drum magazine. Next came the Ameli, made by the Santa Barbara arsenal of Spain, a neat weapon using the roller-delayed blowback system pioneered in the CETME rifle, resembling a small MG42 and belt fed. After that the designs came thick and fast, and the small-caliber light machine gun is now an accepted fact in most armies.

Also in the 1970s, though it was not generally known until 1980, the Soviets had moved to a smaller caliber. Whether this was in response to the American 5.56-mm move, or whether it was simply a progressive step

deduced from ballistic considerations we are unlikely ever to know, but in
1974 the 5.45-mm Soviet cartridge was adopted, and with it a new
Kalashnikov rifle, the AK74. Shortly afterwards this was followed by a
5.45-mm LMG – the RPK74 – which, as might be inferred, was simply a
heavy-barreled version of the rifle provided with a bipod and a larger magazine. But such was the profligacy of Soviet supply that none of the earlier
7.62-mm machine guns was replaced – the new model simply added to
the stocks available.

And now, in the middle 1990s, what can we expect next? As already said,
the design of rifles has reached a point where advance is going to be difficult, and the machine gun might almost be said to be at the same point,
even though there are some options of caliber left to explore. The hunt for
the optimum hit probability continues, however, and the current thinking is
towards a two-barreled weapon, one barrel firing a bullet, the other firing
an explosive projectile. In the US Army this is now referred to as the
"Objective Individual Combat Weapon" or OICW, and the first suggestions
are for a conventional 5.56-mm system co-existing with a new 20-mm
system in the same weapon. The thinking behind this is that the 5.56-mm
rifle will be used when there is a reasonable chance of distinguishing the
target and firing at it successfully – but where the target is indistinct or

**This Spanish soldier fires
the Spanish "Ameli"
5.56-mm belt-fed
machine gun. The barrel
casing resembles the
German MG42 of World
War II, but the
mechanism has more
relationship with the
German G3 rifle.**

Modern sights are no longer pieces of metal with a hole in them. This is the Hughes Thermal Weapon Sight which detects the heat of the human body in light or darkness, allowing accurate aiming day and night.

concealed by cover, then the 20-mm explosive projectile, fitted with a fuse which will detonate it in the air over the target, will shower the area with lethal fragments and thus greatly increase the chance of hitting the elusive target. This poses all manner of technical problems, and it is doubtful whether any practical solution will be seen before the century ends.

Another approach is to improve the "fire control" aspect of the weapon – the sights, the method of acquiring the target, determining its range and calculating the data necessary to direct the weapon accurately. Here, micro-electronics can be brought into play – the techniques for producing a computing sight are well understood and have been used on tank guns for many years, but condensing them into something which will fit on to a rifle or light machine gun is a considerable problem. It has been done, but not in a form small or rugged enough to be adopted for military use. The device consists of a laser rangefinder and a computing micro-chip allied to a sighting telescope. The chip is programmed with the ballistic information regarding the trajectory of the bullet. The firer takes aim on his target through the telescope, placing the cross-wires on it, and presses a button. The laser rangefinder measures the range to an accuracy of five metres, measures it again to confirm, and then passes the information to the computing chip. This calculates the trajectory appropriate to the measured range and then causes the telescope crosswires to move so as to register the correct amount of elevation and drift. The firer now takes a fresh aim, placing the new position of the crosswires on his target, and fires. Unless something unpredictable such as a sudden gust of wind or an earthquake occurs during the bullet's brief flight, the shot should strike the target.

The firearm has come a very long way since its first hesitant appearance in the 14th century – undoubtedly it has a long way to go, though at the present time the path it intends to take is not readily discernible. But this, as we have seen, is really nothing new. The firearm has reached its zenith at several points in the past, and yet it has always managed to make a fresh advance. It may take a year, or it may take another century, but we can be sure that the end of the firearms story has not yet been reached.

Index

Numbers in *italics* refer to illustrations

The publisher wishes to thank the following: Peter Newark's Historical Pictures for pictures on pp 2, 3, 6, 9, 10, 14, 16, 17, 18, 19, 21, 22, 25, 27, 40, 44, 46, 48, 52, 53, 54, 55, 58, 59, 60, 61, 62, 66, 67, 70, 72, 73, 75, 77, 78, 82, 84, 85, 86, 89, 90, 91, 92, 94, 96, 98, 111, 112, 114, 117, 118, 127, 130, 135, 148, 156 and 161; TRH for pictures on pp 102, 103, 107, 110, 126, 134, 138, 139, 144, 146, 147, 150, 154, 155, 158, 164, 166, 175, and 179; Science Photo Library/ Stephen Dalton for picture on p.34 and Ian Hogg for all other pictures.